MW01226279

7c

Thank you!.

Alex

Germain Sainroccó

Defying my Ghosts

Germain Sainroccó

2013

Prologue

I let the fear aside, I faced the ghosts that I loaded for many years, I got brave going over the major and complicated passages of my life from childhood until my first experiences of encounters with older age, I wanted to transfer everything that brought me back memories to paper, before my eyes get tired more than what they are now and before my memory refuses to remember and my conscience distorts the reality. On these pages is no intention of any teaching, I personally learned from my own stories, of my own achievements and failures but it was also necessary to mix my memories with experience over the years that life has given me. Obviously there are situations that I would not repeat and others that I would like to have the opportunity to return to the past to remedy them, as it is impossible to do one or the other I should accept my past as it is and without regrets. Passages that I rescued and snatch not exempt of consequences from the depths of my heart and conscience, passages that I wanted and promised one day to forget, what obviously I did not, perhaps for good. Not everything on these pages is full of joy or total sadness, it is simply life. Thanks to those who are and also, were part of my memories and experiences.

Writing those passages I wanted to also involve my wife and my children, mainly in gratitude for all the happiness, help, understanding, passion and tolerance that I have received from them. For my own sanity I have been cautious not to distort reality, I only mixed objectivity with some touches of fantasy by the simple fact of protecting people who were and are close to me, to avoid running over to those who cannot defend themselves and they will never know that they are part of a story, my story. They will have to respond or be answered, each one according to their own actions, I have not tried to judge or be judged either accuser or accused. My intention has been to just remember and stamping my comments for the moment lived, stage by stage with the mentality of the passing of the years. Evidently not everything regarding my life is here, it would have been tedious, slow and tiring adventures to write and full of secrets that I would have not wanted to share. I do not seek advice on what I should have done or I should stop doing nor giving advice to any of the named here, the reason why these pages do not contain proper names with the exception of a couple of them.

We are all loaded up with secrets and sins and facing them is the true value of life. Forgiveness, when it exists, must be sincere and without conditions. I hope, a day be forgiven by those with whom I acted unjustly.

The earthquake

It seemed a quiet night, although it had been a terribly hot day, hotter than normal for a typical day of summer in Santiago. It began to cede the heat to a gentle breeze, announcing a few clouds in the wide, bright and starry sky. "Tomorrow will be a stifling day", predicted my father, which for me it was a wise judgment that everyone should pay attention. Proud of what has been just said I looked to my younger siblings, who did not pay attention, a day they will understand and may value what dad just said, I thought of an adult form, which at that time it didn't make much difference since I was only three years older than my younger brother. I grew up convinced that my father all knew about life and people, "my father is never wrong", I insisted with my friends and I could challenge them. I told everybody because mom had told me, months before I was born my dad had predicted that I would be a boy, the same thing happened with my sister and then my younger brother, while years later I learned that the true firstborn was not me, the real firstborn had died in the hospital hours after birth. Was my father wrong? No, of course not, that was a doctor's mistake, "the doctor killed him", and how a doctor could kill someone? I do not remember clearly what were the explanations I heard, but there was nothing wrong if dad not insisted on this topic, he had arranged everything in the hospital and dad was not sad when he told me that he had to steal the body of my brother to give burial. Not all parents could expect such feat nor all children may have a father so wise and brave, he knew everything protecting us with his thoughts.

"It is late, it is bedtime, tomorrow will be a long day", said my father. After that we went inside the house, mom remained attentive gaze, like us, without many words to say, dad had all said it. It had been a long day for mom, she had left early to purchase some groceries to prepare lunch, I had been in charge of the house and my siblings, I never will forget that this was my first important day, the responsibility on me, I understood perfectly what concerned with taking care of the house, had been a legacy of my grandparents. I started to walk along the walls that divided our property with the neighbors, mentally counting the bricks of the wall that I was leaving behind, were many, another day I would end that task because I remembered that I had to take care of the house, not to do an inventory of the building, mom had not asked me to do that, but along with counting the bricks I was thinking how much concrete would be necessary to keep together all the bricks in that wall, it wasn't possible by now. The property was big; perhaps another six houses could be built in there. I dared to think that this could be a good business, I would need wood, concrete, bricks, and someone who helps me very closely but what would happen with our yard and our daily games with my brother and sister?, how crazy!, I had forgotten that dad had said he would build a swimming pool. He had everything planned. "Mauricio, Mauricio!" mom was calling me. Had I forgotten my responsibility?, the house was there, intact but what about my siblings? Did they do something wrong while I was walking? No, everything was fine; I was just called by mom to find out where I was.

Among summers, games and dreams I had all, the outside world didn't exist for me or perhaps, I didn't need it. The thick metal gate that dad had built with his hands divided the interior of the exterior, the joy of our family to the sadness of the neighbors and the good from the bad. I could never imagine the "house" without that gate, it was a necessity. What would it happen if the gate wouldn't be there? Impossible! My infancy would not have been the same, I would have been part of the exterior, of the distressed, I'm not sure about the bad guys, but it would definitely not be the same.

"Good night, Mauricio", said mom, kissing my forehead, she also did the same with my younger siblings and turned off the lights.

I shared the room with my younger brother and I always ignored what he said or maybe, I did ignore him totally. It was very important for me to think before sleep, thinking about what I had done and what I would do the next day. It was a simple life, was today, yesterday and tomorrow, the future was tomorrow, after waking up. I was thinking how lucky I was, protected, and nothing could change all that. I fall sleep listening abnormally the dogs howl and bark, why would they do it?

Dad screams woke me up abruptly, I didn't understand what was happening, he ran to my bedroom turning on the lights. My brother jumped from his bed going through the door. I only understood when mom shouted, "Mauricio, run, it is an earthquake!" Not knowing what to do, or where to start, I ran following in the dark the shadows of perhaps my sister. We all met outside, in the courtyard embraced to a small lemon tree. The birds flew in the hundreds quickly drawing shadowy figures in the dark sky. The dogs howled and barked, now with a reason. I could see through the small lemon tree leaves as electricity cables danced fiercely to crash against each other exploding as in a symphony, illuminated by the magic of the sparks as if were fireworks. I think it was in the opposite street from our house that women shouted desperately asking God for forgiveness, how could they have time to ask for forgiveness in those moments? Somewhere glass fell, I think it was all the pottery brought from China by the son of one of our elderly neighbors, poor woman!, it was her greatest treasure, I could not imagine this neighbor drinking tea in a cup of national origin. Dad told me that when people of advanced age begin losing their things that they love; also begin to lose a bit of their life. I could not imagine that Mrs. Zulema was going to die because a few broken dishes, but she died, not really for the love to her pottery but the pottery killed her, a piece of furniture that served as a showcase for her collection fell on top of her. We saw on the other side of our house our neighbors who had no gate, ran rampant through the street, where they would go if we were in the middle of an earthquake? Were fifty five seconds in which none of us said a word, we were mute, terrified at the lemon tree that did not disappoint us. We couldn't see anything because there was no light in the streets or houses but the smell of dust, dry ground in the air mixed with something was engraved in my memory, I never knew for sure what it was, for some time I thought that smell was sulfur, I had heard that when the earth opens that smell comes out to the surface, but I never saw an open land nor I knew that it had been opened before or somewhere.

Slowly we began to move ourselves, to walk, but to where? We were barefoot and there were just piles of debris. The first opportunity that the moon gave me I spotted the countenance of my father, his face was white, I think helped by the light of the moon. The barking and howling of dogs was abruptly changed by the sirens of police cars, fire trucks and ambulances running rapidly through the streets apparently without specific direction. I didn't know what to do, I just looked around us without being able to see anything, I couldn't understand why that happened, of course I came to a conclusion and without being a devout, practicing or faithful believer religious I figured that somewhere had been a great discussion between God and the devil, I never knew who had won that battle because days later people gave thanks to God for this and for that. Some were grateful because they were alive, and others gave thanks to Heaven because another person had died in peace and without suffering.

The sun was already back in the sky, could it be that the moon would have told the sun what happened the night before? I felt much grief to see our neighbors' houses, totally destroyed, just remained to cry their own misery, where would they live now? Who knows, perhaps with some friends or relatives? I heard my father talk with neighbors about the reconstruction, that the government then would do something, send money, aid, food and construction materials. I think it was there where I learned and heard the word "government", all said it, one with respect and others referred to the government with harsh and rude words.

Apparently our house was one of the privileged in our neighborhood, half of the old roof of concrete's shingles went to the ground, the other half of the roof was condemned, two walls of the kitchen also fell destroying part of the stove, furniture and of course, all the pottery but I was not saddened because the earthquake did not destroy any Chinese pottery, I was very confident about it because I never heard mom tell anyone that she loved her pottery, on the contrary, always complained that she had to wash it every day, dry and store it for later return to dirty it. My mother lost an opportunity in her life, an opportunity about to be a millionaire; I remember her telling us why there were no cardboard dishes to be thrown away after use. I also lost that chance because never I paid attention to that idea, years later, I don't know where, someone invented it.

Hours later we could enter in the house, mom cried, we didn't have anything valuable, I think, but she said that it was all lost. Walls inside were broken, the ceiling had fallen on top of the dining room table, beds had a clear color of accumulated dust from the attic, the windows had no glass, the toilet was broken in two. Dad wisely said, "is habitable, I will have to repair the roof and replace window's glasses", giving a silent order to my mother to begin cleaning and sorting the mess left by the earthquake. Dad also added, "The television set seems okay, we'll see when it gets electricity", which took several weeks.

A lot of people died, crushed by their own homes or trying to save something, many died without knowing, in their beds, many were found with unrecognizable faces with money between their stiff hands, many of our acquaintances were included on the lists of the not fortunate.

Perhaps I never sensed everything that we had really lost because we always looked around us, there were many who had lost more than us, there were many who had lost everything and others who had lost nothing but were no longer among us.

Days later again I went through the walls that divided our property to the neighbors; it was a more difficult hike than the original, I had to dribble the large rubble that was in the length and breadth of our yard. I had a broad vision now of what were the houses of my neighbors, I could even imagine their secrets and quickly came to my mind memories of the same people talking, and I could locate them physically among the rubble. None of these houses had been so pretty like ours. Still I felt proud of what we had and we were still having, as the gate of forged metal made by my father's hands, what did not suffer even the scrape in the paint, looked impressive, lonely faced to all fallen, there were no walls to support it, as dad said but it didn't need them, continue straight.

The reconstruction began, the famous government, of which all spoke only gave condolences, sent letters through fiscal employees and of course, many promises. It was expected that international aid arrives so that it could be distributed among the harmed; I don't remember having seen any truck arriving at our neighborhood with materials or food. It was said that other houses in other privileged neighborhoods were rebuilt and years later, officially, the reconstruction process was declared as concluded. What could not be rebuilt or saved was literally destroyed, demolished and used as material for filling. The reconstruction gave way to new buildings and houses, leaving buried the past. Many more earthquakes our house has resisted, which now it doesn't belong to us. I still feel that my childhood was buried under the rubble, many things lost in my mind remained underground and I've never had the courage to rescue them for fear of destroying what little was left of my life. The earthquake opened the borders of my life, at the age of six.

My father was absent constantly from our house, sometimes for days, he said it was a matter of business but my mother was not happy, she began to cry, at the beginning quietly and just tears were running down her cheeks, I remember she said that it was because of the onions she cooked. It seems that my aunts had the same problem with onions because they consoled between them, my mother even cried more. It was very difficult to see my mother as she went down, not laughing with the same joy than before, she no longer played with us, her life became sedentary and constantly looked with pity as trying to ask or answer herself for something, I often asked her what was happening without being answered. Surely must have been the first time that I felt pain, grief and I didn't have anyone who to ask why my heart hurts, it was a deep pain that refused to come out of my body, of my chest and interestingly to me, I began to cry with mom without knowing why, maybe because I didn't understand her grief and she refused to share it with me. I didn't understand why my father wasn't with us and with my mother, to console her, I knew he was working but mom cried and she did it because him, for him, surely. I missed dad because I loved him so much but I was confident that he would soon return and everything would be as before. My father had explained to me that always we would live with the surprises of the nature but I did not understand why he was not with us at that time, and if there is a new earthquake?, who would guide us?, who would give us tranquility as he did with his wise words?

My grandfather, Tata

As I learned later, my grandfather, the father of my mother that I affectionately called him "Tata" had supplied our basic needs. Tata showed much affection, always had an optimistic word to my mother and a smile toward us grandchildren, without counting the bags with food, chicken, cheese, vegetables and more he gave us. I think I was certain that I was his favorite grandson; often he took me with him wherever he could, visit his friends or other family members or simply to walk and talk. He told me a few particulars of his life that fascinated me, I laughed with him so much because its details were anecdotes of when he was young and also when an adult, very funny. Tata was a short man, not measuring more than five feet tall, overweight and bald. Tata once arrived home with a few drinks, it was late and he could not find the key to open the lock of the door, he decided to climb the three steps outside the door, knocked and waited, my grandmother probably slept. As nobody attended Tata began to strongly knock the door until my grandmother awoke but probably scared. My grandmother thought there was a thief trying to enter the house and to surprise the thief and get rid of, she unlocked the door pushing it with force launching Tata a few feet away, then my grandmother called the police which led to Tata arrested but asleep due to his drunkenness. The next day they did not speak, each angry with each other, and with reasons.

Tata tried to explain to me things of adults, such as responsibility, love of family, work, money saving, children and more, he always told me that not everything bad lasts too long, that we must learn from life as well as learning to be patient and understanding of different situations, know how to understand people and learn to forgive. It didn't make sense to me, I was not angry with anyone, nor much less would have to forgive someone; nobody had done nothing wrong to me. Tata looked at me with great sadness and I saw him cry. I don't remember having asked him anything but he responded by saying that many people loved me and I would need to be strong, that it would be time for me to learn.

Tata had worked for many years in lithography for a major newspaper, he explained me what he did daily; mixtures of egg with lemon to make plates in lead or some similar material, I believe that mixture was used as acid to prepare negatives that would printed pages of the newspaper, also Tata could read upside down, he said he had learned it mounting the types or letters in wooden molds to be printed, accommodating from left to right and from bottom to the top, a real negative that could not read or understand by a simple view but when it inked and pressed against the paper it was transferred in all its magnitude the work and effort of Tata with easy-to-read sentences. I remember asking Tata to teach me his craft and expertise, his profession because I wanted to be like him, I wanted to make a living reading upside down showing all that not anyone could do it, my grandfather was my great pride. Tata was disgusted and furious with me, he asked me to never repeat what I had just said, I would not be an employee of nobody breathing harmful acids, working at night, and being humiliated by someone. "You'll be a lawyer, you will make your mother and all of us proud of you, of your efforts, and you will have your own employees who to order", Tata said with great conviction, looked at me with joy, as satisfied that I would do it, it was like a judgment or sealing a pact with someone, perhaps with God. "So will be", he said, taking my hand walking back home.

Tata never mentioned me the name of my father or any comment about him at that time, neither for good nor for bad but I knew they spoke of him, never in front of me or at least knowing that I was close near, rather than comments I only heard his name and consequently I knew they spoke of dad. The time took charge to save many stories, some funny as others less so of the deep friendship that existed between two friends. Tata and dad were very good friends, they say that with more ties to just as father-in-law and son-in-law but they didn't visit each other nor talked, I thought.

Tata did not appear one morning, mom said that Tata had gone to see the doctor because he wasn't feeling well but he would return soon. It passed the day and evening, it rained all night and past more days, mornings and the afternoons looked sad, perhaps because it was autumn and Tata did not even return.

A week later mom asked me if I would like to visit Tata at the hospital, "Of course", I replied exalted, we went out immediately since the hospital was only a block away from our house, it didn't occur to me ask why, what Tata was doing in that cold place, I did not know how to answer me and I left it that way, the answers would come later. I found Tata in a huge room where there were many men of all ages, some slept, others reading and many seemed inert, white as the walls of that gigantic room. Tata was waiting for me with candies and cookies and with a big smile. He took me in his arms and he covered me for a long time, he embraced me with his special fragrance and unique heat, I felt the love entering my blood and my body, giving me all his energy. I felt happy at that moment, I didn't want Tata to say a word, I did not want someone breaking that magic moment, and I realized how much we loved each other. Moments later and breaking that magic time mom said that we would have to leave to let Tata rest. Without pronouncing a word Tata stared me with his small, wet and yellowish eyes giving me the candy and cookies wrapped with his smile. I kissed his cold cheek. "Tata, we will return tomorrow", I said trying to make sure of my promise.

Exactly a week later Tata, my Tata, my grandfather, departed, not as later dad did, Tata had gone to heaven, a violent cancer had attacked him, nothing could be done. Tata insisted with the doctors to send him home after a frustrated surgery to die quietly. He was buried in a sunny day, I remember sitting in front of the gate, waiting for mom. All arrived dressed in black, men and women, my aunts were crying and men embracing each other, there were no children or even my siblings were around. Mom pushed me gently over touching my shoulder, kneeling as if her body was heavy, slowly, she looked sad, sweetly sad, she had already cried so much again, again she had suffered. She told me some details where Tata lived now and that we could go visit him when we would like to.

I said nothing, I had no questions or comments, I think that I had understood everything without reaction, I thought in crying, I couldn't do it, I felt empty, and I was. "Mom", I said, calling her attention and making the only question that came to my mind, "Can I hug Tata again?",

"No", was her answer, short and precise, firm and full of emotion. I never went to the cemetery to visit him. I remember him constantly and I never could forget his face, its special fragrance, his hands holding mine, his unique love, yes, he loved me very much and I did love him too. I've missed him all my life, I still miss him and will miss him until the day that we find each other again, somewhere.

Dad's farewell

Early one morning the main door opened, was daddy, he had returned from his business trip, I thought in just seeing mom's face, she would laugh erasing as by magic the marks on her cheeks by so many tears spilled, those wrinkles that appeared to be permanent, would be watered now by tears of joy. I felt again that pain in my heart but with a mixture of joy, later I would learn and live very closely with these pains; feelings, emotions. Until that time I used to cried because not getting what I wanted or because I had given me a bruise or maybe because I was sent to bed in time that for me was incorrect without counting my erroneous complaints related to the food I didn't like, which were countless; strange combinations like seaweed with legumes and vegetables of all kinds.

My mother had gone out that morning somewhere, she did not alert us where she would go. My father looked at me in a different way, he wasn't affectionate with me or my siblings, and there were no hugs or affectionate gestures, just a look of guilt. How I knew it?, simply, because he looked the same way like when my siblings or I did something wrong, as breaking something important for someone, or lying. I was sure that dad had not broken anything, at least materially. He went directly to his room, took a suitcase and began to pack his clothes, lots of clothes, shoes, all he found. He packed everything he could, everything that belonged to him, like saving his life, his memories, closing, locking and sealing that suitcase as protecting a fortune. I did not understand, dad always said that we would go all together on a vacation trip, to visit and enjoy places but just he was getting ready. "Dad", I said trying to get his attention. "Are we going somewhere?" "Mom has not yet come back", I reminded him. My siblings ran between my father and me without being able to take knowledge of what was happening, also they would not understand whatever that could be but I realized that something was not quite well, there was something strange in the air reminding me his wise words, "Never think or ask in adults' business, you will grow up".

My father stared at me, for the first time there was no expression on his face, I didn't know if he was angry or sad but I was sure that he was not happy and that would leave me sad. I felt guilty and maybe responsible for his sadness by its fixation on look at me without saying a word, accusing me with his look. Today, years later I could not look at him in the eyes, while I have never seen him again, his look of that morning is the memory alive and latent that today I have of my father, that look erased any other of my memory.

"I'm leaving, I want to be happy, take care of your brother, sister and your mother, and now you're a man".

The door closed in front of me, I didn't know what to do, what to think, I was just a kid and my father had given me no option, he let me by inheritance from one minute to another his cowardice, his inability to look at me with love in his eyes and telling me his truth. One second to another left me a spiteful wife and two sons, I would look after myself, I wasn't in his plans as a son and as a beardless that I would have to face life without knowing anything. Breath, think and play was not enough, I should be, or rather; act like a man, be an actor in a real world where I should write the script myself and the actors would be my family, and some time later my father himself. There was no room in that story for a second leading actor.

Mom came a few hours after the "great escape". I told her in details what happened, perhaps not as a narrative, I told her what I thought, felt and would suffer. I demanded her in my immature and healthy judgment to tell me what was happening, she cried for a long time, hugged me and continued crying. My father had left us, had fallen in love with another woman, anyone other than my mother. "He changed us for an adventure", my mother said trying to explain what didn't have an explanation for her, and not much less for us. How my father could have changed a person for a whole family, would he return home?

"You will grow up", had said my father. Many years later I understood what he meant but I understood when I was already grown and matured, not before. At that time I understood his cowardice delivering in other person's hand his responsibility and incompetence of being a father. Indirectly forced me to work and feed my "new" family, at least for me, seen from a different perspective, they were my family and they would remain my family but they were also now my responsibility. My siblings and my mother were like a group of birds in a nest, they did open their mouth to eat or order meal effortlessly. I did grow up, forced by the situation, I did grow up without being asked, and I grew up without understanding it, I grew up without respecting the rules of life, they made me old before being young and they ate my youth.

My nights were not the quietest, in those years I commented that I had many confusing dreams, nobody told me that those were really nightmares. I still remember a very special dream where my father climbed into one of the columns which contained the large gate of our house. After the earthquake it had to be secured so the whole structure would continue standing in full harmony with the rest of what had been barely standing. Getting at the top of the column my father in the dream, fell violently but slowly breaking into a thousand pieces, there was no screaming or blood, only dust in the air which took much time to settle down on the debris, were pieces of clay everywhere. In my dream I tried to put together the pieces and also tried to assemble the figure of my father. Nobody helped me because nobody was there, just me and the pieces that formed the body of my father. I used to wake up scared, what life wanted to tell me through this dream? I remembered the dream constantly trying to find an explanation, which did not come because I normally forgot through the day. I felt much pain to think of my father, I didn't know if this pain was for my father, for my mother, for my siblings or for me or by all. As a child it is very difficult to differentiate who is who and who suffers. I learned that tears were salted, perhaps bittersweet. Are the tears from laughing so much sweeter?

Dreams or nightmares continued, it seemed that every night, I do not remember well but now those nightmares had sound, felt broken the chalks, increasingly more noisy, I never did see my father getting up and I, still looking at the rubble, what more I could have done, he had abandoned me, he had left me alone, I already started in my nightmares to wonder what I should do for my father. There was neither day nor night; it was just that time of the day where it happened, the explosion on contact with the rest of the rubble. The dream had always the same beginning but there was no end, it was just smashing on the floor and I was looking at him without doing something. My comfort or justification was that it was just a dream, only a dream and nothing I could do, just dream it, just keep dreaming it.

My father never called us nor much less visited us, we knew of him by comments of relatives, that had seen him at a party or family reunion, he was fine, he was happy, that his new wife was very pleasant and sociable, that they had adopted a daughter, he had traveled, he did this and that but never a comment about his children and much less about his wife, perhaps an ex - wife, at least I didn't know about it.

A certain occasion a neighbor told me that my father was in a neighboring house celebrating the birthday of one of his friend's son. Three days earlier had been my birthday, my tenth birthday which my mother, celebrated me with tea, bread and margarine, a got a big hug and a kiss asking me to request a wish but there were no guests, no cake and no ten candles, just my siblings and my mother, we were already accustomed to that type of celebrations, we sang and dreamed that a next birthday was going to be a better one than this. There would be cake, gifts, new clothes and guests, a party as God would like to see, said my mother looking at me with his increasingly small and bloodshot eyes in tears, I could no longer read those eyes; I didn't know if those tears were of sadness or excitement of seeing her son grow. It seemed strange to me that only once a year I was treated like a child, I enjoyed it, and I was a little kid again and didn't know until when this would last. Many years later I had problems remembering my birthday, it was difficult to me divide between reality and fantasy, my best birthday parties were in my mind, no photos, there were no gifts, there were no guests, there were no memories, only my fantasies.

After some time, I don't remember clearly how much time had passed, but I do remember that it had been a painful time with many needs, and my father was celebrating a party for other people, in my small mind to a more fortunate child than me but I felt no envy of my neighbor. I spied my father for a couple of hours, he came out of the party heading to a main avenue to get a taxi, I went to confront him but I didn't know what to tell him, how to face him, at the end he was my father and he had rights over me even though they were abusive. He entered a bar, probably he took a half of an hour inside, he left the bar and extending his arm did stop a taxi, he got inside closing the car's door firmly. I didn't realize that had lowered the glass window looking at me, again, as some years back, I did approach slowly and fearfully to the taxi and him. "What do you want?", "Money!", I answered, "Something to buy food, still not have eaten tonight", I insisted. I wanted to tell him a million things on his face, I felt rage, and I felt helpless. He stared at me regardless sitting inside his taxi, had started to rain and I was there, unprotected, begging to my own father for some money. Suddenly I felt that my stomach turned, I felt revulsion, and I felt selling myself to the worst bidder. I noticed my wet face and wanted to know if it was the rain that began to fall stronger in that moment, and I knew right away and from my own past experiences that rain was not salty, again I was "eating" my tears. I didn't want to cry but I could not speak. The salt of tears had left me silent. My father smiled, put his hand into a pocket and threw a coin as if in slow motion, it shone in the air and fell to the wet sidewalk, I took it and I kept it. The taxi moved away quickly without giving me the opportunity to understand. I went to the emporium that was still open despite the hour; I bought flour, everything that coin could pay for. I got home, my mother was worried about the time, was late, my siblings fall slept on the couch, I prepared a bread with flour, water, salt and some oil and I put it to cook slowly in a skillet. We ate and we went to bed, there were no questions or answers or even comments, we ate in silence, in my mouth the bread had a different taste, salty, really salty, tears run without control on my face. Early in the morning I woke up with the feeling of having drunk too much water, sea water, all the water from the sea, salty, very salty. That morning my nightmare made sense, was simpler than I imagined, see falling and shattering on the floor my idol, now it was just mud, fell over and over again, shattered again and again, I had finally decrypted why I was waking up tired, worried and with fear, which harmed me so much, I should not longer be worried about those foreign falls. I should not longer care if it was raining and the rain melted the clay and mud. I felt safe for the first time in my short life, I felt safe, dry, protected but also humiliated, offended and abused. It was one of the many ghosts that I would continue having in my lifetime, which I would prepare myself to fight, I didn't know how but I had to prepare myself, I should make my skin a leather lizard and my soul invisible, where nobody, ever, would try to destroy me. My dreams were now another.

A violent country

I worked hard during the day and studied in the evenings, all that sacrifice bore fruit, we were not living like kings nor as homeless people, we were still being poor but we had access to hot and decent food, clean clothes and sweet taste to walk with pride where neighbors or relatives pointed us with their fingers reminding us of our sufferings as if we had been the perpetrators, at least they had forgotten our life, of our problems, our misfortune. I turned the page, not easily but I had succeeded, my mind was busy about the future, now I could understand many things, analyze them and take decisions for me and for my mother and siblings, they were still my responsibility. As a young man I had political and social positions, I talked and explained with my classmates my positions and was also reprimanded by my teachers. They say that a child should not speak on those issues that were reserved for adults, what they knew about my life and my experiences?, I did not answer them simply because I would have to give explanations of which I would not feel comfortable, of my experiences that they didn't care and how a young man had more experienced life than the rest without any fear to comment anything. I learned to be silent, I learned to hear, and I learned to speak when it was necessary, for my own benefit. I turned may be a selfish person, perhaps I learned to not worry about the rest, as it would have been possible to do so if the twenty-four hours per day were already short for me. I didn't have enough time to give me some goodness of life such as trips or festivities, my life was working, studying and meet my family needs, keep everything running at home, going with mom to do shopping, attend my brother and sister, listening them and mainly treat them as children, what they were. They wanted to play, run, jump, and climb trees. They wanted to paint, they wanted to understand why was raining and why had sunny days. They cried, laughed and dreamed about Christmas and suddenly when it was least thought they had fallen slept, just in time to take them to their beds, I had no more answers. It was so much that I had yet to learn.

It was 1973, Chile had become a violent and intolerant country, began to lose respect for people and their property, there was much fear in the air and everyone had an opinion and a prediction of what could have happened, I had mine too. But we were wrong, all of us. Obviously many supported the leftist government and the other half condemned by all the problems that appeared daily; lack of food, lack of fuels for vehicles, for public and private transportation, for tractors in the fields, oil for heating used also in stoves in our houses. Lack of medicines, lack of toilet paper and more, there was nothing and if it was, nobody knew where the products were stored. The government decided to ration everything including what wasn't available by delivering to each family a control card to buy basic necessities. A half pound of sugar and a couple ounces of cooking oil could have been for a Monday and Tuesday a roll of toilet paper and a pound of flour and a few cans of cabbage with chopped hot dogs called "Chinese rolls" coming from China. If a person had political contacts, evidently at low level, it was not necessary to disturb the big ones by something that they did not recognize as a real problem, could opt for a double ration or even delivered at home in the dark hours of the night, an award for being loyal "partner". It was a difficult time to live but on the other hand we had much money available, I didn't care if I had to replace anything at home or pay more for something on the black market, I had money, enough in my pocket as everyone in Chile. Soon I discovered that the money would no longer buy anything, turned to be just paper, without any value. It was a circus; now looking back I realize that it was a circus with millions of clowns acting, on both sides. We lacked painting our faces to celebrate as real clowns, some said it was protesting but I believe it was defending. Almost all of Latin America had fallen into the same political and social play and coincidentally at the same time. I heard news that Brazil, Uruguay, Argentina and many other countries were more controlled citizens than us, with more future but also there was news considered clandestine that spoke of repression. I didn't care, I lived in Chile and was a Chilean citizen and our day to day was to make more lines in the market to get our basic needs. Sometime later I thought it was funny in thinking that we did lines without knowing what was being sold; bread, noodles, oil and more, it became customary, that was our life.

I was going to turn fifteen years old in June and decided to celebrate in the way I had never before done. I wanted my family, relatives and friends and we prepared a party buying the necessary items in the famous lines and on the black market too. It would be a great party as I never had before, they would bring me gifts and we would share talking, dancing. Perhaps I wanted to prove to everyone or even more to myself that I was no longer a child, and was not. Mom worked quite so much to come out all right for my birthday party, she cleaned windows and doors, she waxed the hardwood floor throughout the house, she did shine the dining table and furniture, she prepared new table cloths, she made new clothes for my brother and sister and for her too, it was all ready for the next day. It was now just to wait, I felt very strange, it was the first time in my life that had so much attention from all, that made me remember five years earlier when I spied my father at the birthday party of our lucky neighbor, now it was my turn, my turn to celebrate and share with those who I wanted, maybe not with those who deserved but I also needed guests and of course, their gifts. It was a long night in which I could hardly close my eyes, I was really nervous and worried about the hours passing quickly so I decided to go back in time, forcing memories and analyze everything that I had gone, I felt lucky to have reached fifteen years old safe, I felt even more than fortunate, a lucky person. The time that was happening in my life, the accumulated day by day was helping me to mitigate the past, the bad memories do not hurt so much but they were there, it was very similar to a situation that I lived when I was little, playing with my cousins, I fell down sitting in a glass jar in the garbage can that mom had put at the end of the back yard so that nobody could have an accident. I cut my thigh and I had to be carried to the emergency room, thirteen stitches in a vulgar seam, rude as a sack of potatoes. It became a great scar that does not hurt but it is a mark. I have always compared this fact into my life, no longer hurts, but it is there.

I woke up very early on June 30, was a Saturday and the country was in a panic and total alarm, the previous day, Friday 29 occurred the infamous "Tancazo", famous for us Chileans and unforgettably for me, obviously. An attempt of coup d'état against the President and his government, the curious name of the tancazo was the reason that army tanks took to the streets trampling everything that was on the road, I remember that a tank rolled over a citroneta, a French car that looked like a frog, squashing altogether, the poor vehicle ended not average more than two feet high. The people, the population in general was worried and very scared because the tancazo had been a message from the armed forces to the government, to its supporters and citizens in general. The future situation did not look good and the present was untenable. The worst part of the tancazo was my missed birthday party, there was no party, the guests did not arrive nor much less my gifts. Mom was very sad for me, there were many sacrifices and expenses to no one appear, I had doubts if someone had planned to go to my party, probably not. We began to celebrate, mom, my siblings and I around six o'clock in the evening. We ate and play, there were no gifts but they were also not necessary, that was what I felt at that moment. I felt happy because I was celebrating with those who loved me, I felt happy and I was.

The coup d'état

September 11, 1973, nobody could leave their homes, shot from all sides, it was confusion and chaos. Nobody went to work or to school, policemen and armed forces' trucks ran and howled swiftly through the streets sowing tension and panic, they did not respect traffic lights, traffic signs nor much less civilians who ran desperately in front of them causing more panic. I got the impression that they, the uniformed, didn't know where they were going, their faces reflected disruption, concern, no valid information was available and I believe neither of nor for them, just speculation. Television stations aired the information nervously what they could but the few available news was unfounded and unsupported. Radio transmissions were a little different, more dramatic news and soon they become one by one silent by the "official" guidelines. With the intention of finding any indication or direction of what was happening, what was very difficult, we were playing side to side with our radio's dial looking for something, like holding by a thread of hope that everything would end shortly, Chile and Chileans had suffered enough already. Suddenly and from nothing we heard a deep and very calm voice, the voice of the President of Chile, was a short message, I remember it every day better, I recorded it in my head forced by my own insistence. In those tragic moments I engraved a phrase the President uttered, marked in some part of my brain and minted into fire, *"Know all, that sooner than later, the large avenues will be opened again where the free man will walk to build a better society"*. I had understood the fragility of a system, of any system, anywhere where the avenues and streets could be closed, drowned to the most vulnerable class, the working class who suffer because the fortunate is contrary to the voice of the people and contrary to the free voice of a society or called society in what we assume that we should live under the same roof of rights, a responsible government, peace and justice, legally and socially. I knew and understood later that closing an avenue meant the imposed silence to speak and to an opinion, to act and demonstrate, the same stiffness that Chile had thrown away because of so-called pseudo politics, inept, corrupt and insatiable of money, position and power. We pay for years, and very expensive by our own errors, we began to feel it immediately and we pay for it not only the unfortunate as also the fortunate, what some called and still call traitors. The time would be responsible for writing or maybe rewrite history.

There were long years of sorrow and silence, many were the dead, which I saw on the street or floating in a river. Congress was closed and they fired all the representatives of the people, were installed new mayors in all places to represent the new government, for certain, all military, many colleges, universities and high schools were taken to control due to the strong political influence, the Constitution was suspended, by decree were suspended all political parties, mainly those of the opposition, trade unions were abolished and censored the press in general, among other measures. Not even hospitals with their medical directors were saved, were appointed more military to manage them, at the end everything was under strict military control, the dictatorship had installed to stay. The laws were new and were published every day enacted by the military junta or government representing the four branches of the armed forces; army, marine, aviation and police, these laws were absolutely to suppress any attempt at protest, re-establishment of rights and of course, to the fixed, attentive and the accusatory international view. Many countries turned a blind eye to violations of human rights, to the minimum rights, the right to speak, to manifest ourselves, and more importantly, the right to live.

Many countries punished us with economic embargoes, and we paid the consequences once again, countries justifying their actions for our sake, countries who called us friend and "brother country", according to them. I questioned the word brotherhood for a long time, because I had questioned myself many times the words father and son on many occasions but not brother. No one could travel to any place on the planet without first having a travel authorization issued by international police, the civilian police. Many times this was denied or postponed until a deeper analysis; it was not otherwise an inquisitive regarding to the whole family. If someone had a surname that would coincide with an enemy of the new government, it was a problem, a serious problem not just by leaving the country as well as in traffic controls and street controls where any member of the government and the police could stop anyone, asking for documents and retain. The Prussian-style settled quickly, men should demonstrate total masculinity, with short hair and shaved; otherwise men were humiliated been kneeling down them and cutting off their hair in public roads at gunpoint, not precisely in any saloon. Children, young people and adults were treated in the same way, without respect, there were no apologies. One of our neighbors of about sixty years old used to wear his hair longer than normal to cover a scar as a result of a car accident, on an occasion we were going toward the center of the city in his car when a group of soldiers made us stop and descend the car, without any question they pointed a gun while another soldier behind cut his hair showing great joy and of course, power. My neighbor shed a couple of tears when reflected his face in a window, obviously by feel humiliated than losing his hair or having to show from now on the scar. My impatience was so great that I could not stand in a comment to the soldier, "I'm glad that Jesus no longer walks on Earth nor less in Chile", I said, to which the soldier replied, "Keep praying". There were no consequences due to my comment because my neighbor pushed me into the car.

Women were abused the most, they should dress as such, soldiers ordered them to remove their pants leaving them in underwear and let them go their way in that condition, Chilean women should dress skirt, dress. Help? Under no circumstances! Could be possible that the soldiers and officers had no family; parents, children, sisters?

Homosexuals also suffered, many of them paid with their own lives, the government had no sympathy for them. Homosexuals normally at that time were engaged in the business of beauty, their businesses were traditionally located in the downtown of Santiago and after the military coup and its social consequences those businesses were empty, their owners disappeared or went into hiding or perhaps dissimulated. It was dangerous to speak the truth, we were taught to lie. Chile has always been a conservative country and discriminator, homosexuals or simply mistakenly called at that time and by all of us fags, where the negative part of the society and the shame of any uniformed, it was necessary to put an end to what God has not commanded nor ever approved, I imagined that in the whole world would be the same. The same killers would prove and would give the reason to the world that the real fags were those thinking that had the right to keep the people silent, to change and transform people with rifles loaded with hatred and terror in situations where political color was not a factor and no less a danger to the new society to be built.

The red color was literally forbidden and mainly in freight trucks, the red color represented communism. The military government continued its struggle against communism, Marxism, Leninism, as said the General and also what did not exist or was difficult to prove for any ordinary citizen. The uniformed forces forced the entry in churches, trade unions, schools and companies, they always found weapons; sub-machine guns, bombs, knives, Nunchaku and "miguelitos" made with nails to destroy the vehicle's tires, I wondered how the nuns of the convent might have acted so subversively.

The ambition of power also came to the heart of the military junta, the General proclaimed himself as President of the Government's junta, Commander in Chief of the armed forces, general captain of five-star and President of the nation of course, of which I remember. The people proclaimed him dictator. I think the only thing that could saved him letting the doubt in the vast majority of the population was his excessive zeal to defend the country against communism and his honesty but everything went down when began to appear clandestine cemeteries, lists of disappeared detainees, violations of human rights and later, years later, after his death to be more precise was found a fortune deposited in different international banks of friendly countries and "brother countries", that would have been impossible for any general or even for any president of any country accumulate millions in a honest way. All good theories were muddy, stained due to greed and lust for power. It is said that we all have a price, we do not come with a label with a value but we know it when we sell ourselves, when it is late.

Today, after so long, the ghost of the division remains between us, we still wonder what happened, how to prevent it to happen again, knowing already the answers. We still divided into two groups, the against and in favor, those who are looking for their dead and those who ask to forget, those who suffered and those who appreciate, those who ask and those who prefer silence, those who are still crying and those who celebrate, those who promise revenge and those who repeat the same mistakes, those who promise not to mistake again and those who promise war, those who abuse of democracy and those who warn not to do so, those who say that we learned and those who say that we are still ignorant. We all still suffer, some lost more than others but we all lost something, in a war there are no winners, only losers. We have not learned to open the avenues, it frightens us face reality, if it seems that polarize would be a good choice; the freedom of some does not mean that freedom is for everyone.

Were seventeen years of dictatorship, seventeen years in which children and young people paid the consequences for adults' errors, regardless if the adults were left or right wing. We, the youth got to have no ambitions, they cut off our wings and we lived day and night with fear, insecurity and suspicious of our own shadows, and we were the future of Chile.

The only hope that many saw was leave that rarefied and dangerous environment searching for a new world, fresh horizons where we learn to feel a value for ourselves, to feel important, to dream of the chance of a new life, with a job that was not wearing a military uniform. Many did and many of us followed different paths.

I think have not been with any trauma that dictatorship could have left in me, each one must analyze their own life and their own truth, pains of wounds go away, the pains get calm thanks to the unquestionable passing of time but the scars are never erased, one of the scars I will carry with me, forever, and one of them became a phobia; I tremble and I shudder every time I see a policeman, I feel fear, to the point of feeling funky pounding of my heart transformed into an arrhythmia, I feel my mouth demanding water and the lack of control of my hands trembling as wanting to flee. Yes, afraid, very afraid.

Knowing my family

What to do? Where to go? Those were just questions into the air that would not have evidently an answer. It was like living in a bubble, vegetating and waiting for the good fortune give us a miracle, a decent job, a sense of life that feed our souls. Nobody laughed and there was no reason to do so. I was fifteen years old and had no future and was hungry to learn, to travel, to be important to myself, and I was, since I had to maintain my mother and my younger siblings and they rested on me. My dreams and aspirations became background and it was no sacrifice, it was almost automatic, I only did it because there were no other doors, other alternatives, other opportunities. I knew that I had grown up, not more crying, nor bitterness and pain. I learned to live, absorb and mimic pain, to live with the bitterness of others, already the tears of my mother did not longer affected me, it hurt me yes to see her cry, it hurt me yes see her falling into her depressions that increasingly were more frequent but I couldn't, I should not think of me, I knew that I was doomed to be slaves by my own choice or perhaps the comfort and cowardice of someone else than me. They were just dreams, nothing more than that, my future was referred to just a dream and I should not change the law of my life; I was convinced that I could dream but just that and dreaming within limits.

As if it had been something forbidden, I used to read at night or when travelling to work or school, tourism magazines, that was my secret. Photos of beautiful places, beaches, mountains, rivers, snow and people having fun, children laughing, men fishing and hunting, women taking a drink into flashy glasses adorned with colorful umbrellas, oranges and olives, all in different colors, children and young people with sodas in their hands, bottles of different colors and flavors for each one of them, and everyone laughing. It fascinated me to see those pictures, they were happy people and I enjoyed seeing happy people, people that only existed in those magazines, it was as if you were seeing a magazine of the future with the absolute assurance that one day this would be true, true as interstellar travel would exist.

Time went through, a couple of years passed and I began to feel old, tired. One day I looked myself in the mirror and I saw gray in my hair, it glistened in the light, a boy of seventeen years with reeds, I could hardly believe it. I could not compare me with anyone else since I was the oldest of my siblings and the older person at home was my mother and she had a uniform color without gray hair. How could it be? I remember that weekend I decided to stay at home, doing nothing, just sitting watching the routine of my mother and my siblings. How strange they were to me, I felt invisible because no one exchanged a single word with me, I only heard comments and conversations, and all had plans for that night. My sister screamed from her room that she was going to spend the weekend with her friends from school and mom had authorized it. My brother asked me if I could take him to a cousin's house a few blocks away, I agreed. When he was ready he handed me his bag with some clothes and toys so we headed towards our cousins' house. Half-way started to exchange some words with him, "are you tired, thirst?" I asked, "Yes", he replied. We stop at a soda fountain, I bought two soft drinks and we sat down. The night was warm running a nice breeze, my brother quickly emptied his soda as that someone would snatch, he had not totally finished it when he asked me for one more, and I bought it. "How school is?" I asked, "I think well", he said. "Do you need something?" I asked, "Like what?" He answered quickly without giving me time to think. "I don't know, something you need, something that you would like to have", to my surprise he took a long time and finally said, "No, nothing, perhaps a new friend for mom, who would treat me better, it seems that he does not like me". "A friend?", "What are you talking about?", I asked curiously, "Mom told me to not tell you but she has a friend". I thought asking mom a thousand questions, I had many mixed feelings. I felt rage, grief, disappointment, betrayed, pain. Why mom would need a friend? Mom cried so much on my shoulders and how much I had mourned her own cry? "Let's go", said my brother, "I want to go with my cousins, we have to play". Again I took his bag with his toys and clothes and we began to walk, my brother took my hand, which had never done before, I squeezed his hand forcefully and he didn't say anything, he just watched me, perhaps understanding my pain. At that moment my soul burned because I understood what he needed, he wanted love and I had not given it, at least in the quantity and quality that he had wanted to, there was emptiness in his heart that I could not fill it. On that walk we did not exchange more words I could understand and perhaps, I did see the future of my younger brother, it was already marked, he would grow up marked by the lack of affection and love. What would be about him? What could I do? Time would give me reason, unfortunately. When we arrived I hugged my brother strongly and for a long time, I kissed him on his cheek without saying a word, I didn't know what to say and the words were unnecessary at the time.

That was the last time I would see that innocent child's face, not because he changed in a short time, but again because something changed in me, the way in which I saw things, situations and people. I walked slowly back home, thousands of thoughts flooded my mind trying to review my life in shooting stages, I wanted to delay my arrival at home as I could, I got no intention to confront mom, I didn't want to talk, words weighed so much that I could hardly put any sentence out of my mouth. Fortunately the house was in the darkness, there was no one, neither mom nor my sister were at home, they had left, where? It didn't matter.

I walked into the darkness of the yard, which I had traveled many times; I sat in a corner, nestled between the black of the night and the shadows of the trees. I felt alone, as lonely as the stars in the infinite, I thought of asking the sky everything that concerned me but I felt ashamed to speak and even thinking. Who would answer me? What if the answers were not of my satisfaction? It seemed than more I looked at the sky more stars appeared to shake and dance in harmony, the lights went and returned as a math problem, according to the logic, the unknown of the lights absorbed me and I thought to be in the middle of them, where the most important thing was not to ask nor to speak, maybe just to exist. I knew that many stars up there were already dead but they had left light traveling through the infinite and forever, I wanted to be a star at that time, I wanted to be a light, I wanted to be someone or something, suddenly I wanted to be happy. I would need my own space to project my own light, that which I had inside me, the light that had never illuminated. I got tired of loneliness; I got tired of sadness and darkness of the soul.

I decided that my presence was not longer needed at home; I didn't want more sad afternoons, or long days with my endless nights. Didn't make sense to ask mom what she thought, she would tell me that she needed me to live, to pay the bills but I needed me, I needed to love me, to understand me, I needed to live, much more than breathing, I needed to stop victimizing me, I needed to see and understand life from within my being. I needed to separate the reality from fantasy and dreams. I needed to find out my own answers, not what somebody would tell me, I needed to hear and see for myself what life would have to tell and show. I didn't think for a second how much this decision would cost me but I thought that I have also the right to exist and to be happy. Yes I would, I was doing it, I was taking the first step in my life and own decision, there I would head to my light.

Mom's reaction was harder than what I imagined, "Selfish, bad brother, ingrate son!" And the more she imagined in telling me. At that time I thought that it was good that she insulted me and, I wanted, more, I asked silently, just to justify my decision to go since I had not been selfish or bad brother and much less an ingrate son, I had given my life for them but I also wanted her to vent out. She cried for a long time and asked the sky the reason for my decision; mom looked at me with pain, directly in my eyes, "Why?" I had many answers, motives and reasons to explain why but I chose to keep quiet, we didn't need to get into conflicts, my decision was already taken. Days later I went back to talk to mom, I tried to explain my point of view, I reaffirmed that I loved her, also my brother and sister, I wanted to live and not die in life, why I didn't have the right to my future? "No", was her categorical response, you don't understand, she repeated again and again. Calmer now, she tried to explain to me the inexplicable, I was biting my lips avoiding to respond. I always treated mom with much respect and there was no reason not to do so but my response at that time, my final answer deserved a different voice tone to put an end to that absurd discussion, I thought about it and I had told my own interior hundreds of times. I slowly got up from my chair, crossed my hands in front of me and calm, very calm and firm voice I said, "It is time that you assume your role as a mother, you have left two sons, this adoptive father got tired", she hugged me, I didn't know if she was crying but she let me go, in peace.

I never knew other details nor I asked mom about her friend, I didn't want to know, mom never again married or redo her married life, she still lives for them, for my brothers and by her grandchildren, unfortunately an estrangement still lasts between us and my own family, she has her favorite grandchildren that are not my children but she loves her favorites. If she could not be the best mother in her youth she learned to be a very good grandmother in her old age, it is not the same thing?

Many things went through my head but for good, I felt free, I felt young and went back to being young. I don't think having thought of consequences, I had taken certain precautions as giving enough money to my mother for some time expenses. Deep in my being I had the certainty that my mother was physically and mentally suitable for working and she did so, she began to produce and sell clothes to her closest friends and relatives at home to later specialize in Haute Couture, she enjoyed it, delighted, spending her own money, saving and making plans. I enjoyed it very much, to the point of emotion when I knew of her achievements, I was proud of mom, all of us were, and she wouldn't depend financially on nobody in her life, not even from me. Mom never forgave me for having abandoned them by my selfishness, sadly it was not important for me what she thought of me, I already had done what my conscience dictated to me. No doubt at that point in my life I was more important than anyone else, I had no doubts and no one would have more importance than I. Yes, maybe I had become selfish.

I had gathered money secretly for a long time, it wasn't much but it for me was a small fortune, it was enough to finance my plans. I felt fear and concerned about having so much money in one of my pockets by twenty-four hours a day but I knew that I could not touch it; nothing would justify any spending, nothing. Days later walking through downtown, I found myself staring in a shop window, I went back to reality because of the vision in the thick glass, it was my own face reflected, a child with eyes hugely open and injected of curiosity and the mouth a little more than open, there was nothing supernatural, only a toy, the most wonderful of all, in all its glory; It was a race car track set, black as a freshly paved road and two race cars positioned in their tracks, one red and one blue, the remote controls to one side as inviting a dreamer like me, to be activated. It must have measured more than seven feet long by three wide. I suddenly jumped back, someone was bringing me back to reality touching my shoulder, somewhat uncomfortable I turn my head to look at who dared in putting an end to that intense moment of pleasure, I had never seen that kind of... toy, not even in my journals of tourism in which I knew part of the world and its wonders, in illustrations for advertising. Uncomfortable I turned around and I started to walk away from the big window, the same man followed me with a friendly smile, he invited me to return to the glass, I came back, not very confident. "Do you like it?" He asked kindly, there was no other answer than yes, unless I was lying, I did not. "Do you want to come inside and test it?", "Is very fast and good quality, we just got it, it is imported". I accepted immediately, both were looking at it carefully, at least I studied it and I wondered silently, how works it? I didn't think that the seller thought of something else that in making the sale, his position made me think that he was very proud of owning something so fantastic, the man took the controls extending me one, I accepted and prior to accommodate it and adjust it to my hand I strongly squeezed the trigger, my little electric car flew through the air, I followed it with my scared sight and asking for it should land somewhere gently and safe, it crashed against the countertop following his mad march to a stop inside a garbage can. I felt ashamed of looking at maybe the offended owner of the track; I started to leave the control when I heard his laugh, strong and contagious behind me. "Do you see the force that has? You must be careful to avoid accidents", he said and added, "Do you take it?" How could I say no? "How much it does cost?" It was the only thing I said. The price corresponded to the fourth part of my little fortune, the truth is that I recalculate my accounts quickly and as by miracle they reconciled and if it would have cost the third part of everything I had in my pocket I had bought it anyway, it had no price for me and my numbers should reconcile in the same way, the tracks had to be mine. I walked carrying out the huge box, several people watched me curiously, other envious and I felt pleasure in seeing those faces with signs of disgust, I thought a thousand things, I would have liked to read everyone's thinking, what they looked at?, What they thought? It took not much until a woman made the most negative and mean comment while I waited for a taxi to take my new treasure, "That is throwing money away!", It hasn't affected me and I felt much joy, I smiled and I laughed, I cared not surprise nor upset by laughing in her face. I knew very closely envy because I had felt it all my life but I learned to live with it, I never let it get out of me, I controlled it, I was always in command of all of my feelings and emotions.

The old painted black and yellow cab stopped in front of me, the driver lowered the window asking if I wanted to put the box in the trunk, my refusal sounded somewhat violently, "No, thank you", I repeated calmed, I acted like someone outside was going to steal my tracks. I gave him the address where I wanted to go; he nodded his head giving understood to my instructions. "Is it for your child?" The driver asked. I quickly remembered that I showed older than I was. "No, it is for a child", I replied. Soon we got home, I paid the service of the taxi, the driver receiving the money offered me good morning but not without first making his last comment, "Your child will be happy".

Nobody at home, it was perfect. I opened the box and I begin to assemble all parts of the tracks, after some minutes it was ready, it was mine, only mine. I sat down front to it asking me that I had done, I remembered that some time back I had bought a can of condensed milk, I went to the back yard and I finished it, all, every last drop, I did not share it. The next day I had stomachache, headache, arcades, nausea and vomiting. A couple of days later I was recovered from the stomach but not of my conscience. Trying to justify my recent purchase, I had never had a toy nor much an expensive one like that, now I had it, I had succeeded but it would not get me closer to what I lost as a child, it would not bring me back all the missed Christmas nor much less my absent birthday parties. I had at that moment what I never had before but it did not fill me the soul, on the contrary, I felt great sadness, time had been unforgiving with me without greater notice, without more opportunities, I was no longer a child.

The door opened, my brother stared at the new toy, he ran, hugged me and I thanked many times as if I had bought it for him. Let's play he said, and we play for a long time, mom watched from a corner trying to understand what was happening. The hours passed and my brother fell asleep. "And now, are you going to take the toy with you?", "No mom, it is for my brother and I don't want to talk or explain anything, you would never understand it". "I prefer that you take it", she insisted, "I imagine it's something very expensive", she said. "Yes, it is true, it is quite expensive but having seen the face of happiness in my brother, it has no price", I said and insisted, "did you know mom that at least two people are needed to be happy?". "Why you are saying that, are you not happy?" She said, challenging. "No, I'm not happy, that I have certainty, and why I should be happy?", "Is there something to celebrate?" Happiness is a celebration of life, must find a reason to be happy.

The departure

I had requested a visa to travel to the United States, and also a ticket in the air force, the ticket was approved, not before without moving some contacts and ask for favors to some fortunate that everything they could but it didn't matter, I wanted it and needed it. To my surprise the visa to enter the United States was denied, the brotherhood said no, I personally went to the Consulate to understand the refusal, I did not receive any response, the borders were not only lines on maps. Many friends and their families traveled to different countries of the world, almost all citing political reasons, most exiled, it was not an option for me. Argentina, Peru, Bolivia? Bordering countries, they weren't a real alternative, economically and socially they were in a worse situation than Chile, they were governed under the weapons also. The doors of opportunities were closed quickly and time passed by and there were not options, I did hit many doors, I read everything that was possible finding an answer, I visited many consulates including the Vicarage of Solidarity and Caritas

Chile, both depended on the Catholic Church, the answers and tips I received were not encouraging, all had major problems than me, or better said, real problems.

A few days later I got a visit, an acquaintance to me, he was the nephew of a man who lived in Brazil for many years and he was looking for someone who could help him to drive back to Brasilia after a long vacation, it was a trip of three days, very tiring and dangerous for one person only. He had had many problems in his initial trip so he decided to seek help. More interesting than its idea was according at what I was looking for, I never thought in Brazil, it seemed so distant, so incognito, and so tropical, I didn't think about it twice, I said yes. I wanted to know the details of the future adventure but my questions echoed in all people, nobody knew or didn't want to know, and at the end all had their own questions to their own problems and no answers. I resigned to wait, will come the day that the trip began, was my comfort. It was a Monday afternoon, "We will depart tomorrow at dawn" was the message, I felt fear and thousand worries stalking my mind, hundreds of questions nailed like pins in my head, I didn't know how to react, the news gave me a total blank, and I do not remember when I returned to reality.

The farewell was quick, devoid of any scene really emotional and even pain, it was a goodbye than a farewell without greater emotion, must have been some of tears from my mother to what my brothers possibly imitated. I believed I knew how I was going but I didn't know if someday I would be back, of what I was sure was I had no plans nor deadlines in time to return, return to what?

I remember having felt a severe pain in my stomach that lasted some days, it seemed like a wound but calming slowly, very slowly as an open wound healing, I got to thinking that the umbilical cord had broken, the pain of the soul was stronger than the pain of my stomach, I did the impossible to not cry and I did not cry but tears ran uncontrolled down my cheeks like drops of rain, as pearls burning and I felt sad, my conscience weighed more than my own body. "It is normal, don't worry", said my new friend who was driving through the plains of Argentina heading to Brasilia, I could not respond because I didn't know what to say, neither to him nor myself. His comment was circling in the air for a long time, maybe years. How it could be possible feel nostalgia, grief, bitterness, affliction, it's the feeling of guilt and condemnation, that feeling of punishment. Of course, it was not normal in my limited understanding and the chained distance to my destiny began to charge minute after minute the distance between my world and the new world diminished increasing my memories between the point where I was at that moment with my memories, with my childhood, as the life I had, the only life that existed for me, the only life I knew. Maybe I called it lives because I wanted to make a big difference between my lives, my joyful life, the future would show me which I imagined and my life I had just left. I'd have time to gather all my live in one.

"What are your plans?, where you will live?, how you will live?, do you bring enough money?" I was shot by the questions. Again, I was there receiving the warm air on my face, it was summer and Argentina's flatland did not have mercy, hard heat! Silently, without answers to my life, to my present and much less, to my future. No, I didn't have enough money, I had not thought about it too, much less I knew where

I was going to live. Why I would need plans if I had lived all my life without plans, the day by day would teach me and it would give me the answer, just faith, it was everything I had, faith that there would be a roof for the rainy nights, conviction to find shelter from the sun, confidence in a helping hand that would give me a piece of bread, and a bag with some pieces of old, worn clothes, a toothbrush with old bristles and a jar with baking soda for toothpaste's replacement and at the same time to be used as a deodorant. I did not answer my new friend, simply because I had no answers, there was nothing to answer, I even did not look at him, my silence was my accomplice of my truth, he understood it well, I imagined, because that day there were no more questions.

Later in the day and when the sun fell meekly and its last dozy rays changed the reality on the horizon making everything dance in shades of red, orange and yellow, the car stopped, "I'm going to eat something, I'm tired", said my new friend disappearing behind a dusty door of the small and old restaurant that was next to the road, the tiny building and vehicles parked around seemed trimmed from an old magazine, it was all so unreal the time and space, all painted in an amber tone. I got out of the car slowly as asking permission to my legs to move, they did not respond as I would have liked, I felt my clumsy body, my head weighed much, I felt dizzy and breathing was difficult due to the excessive heat and concentrated moisture in the air, the feeling was like breathing sand, it's been so many hours sitting motionless, just the foreign running of the car. I hardly walked into the restaurant and let my body fall into a chair next to my friend, he was eating meat and salads in an almost desperate way, he gave me a quick and prosecuting look by stretching out his hand to wrest the single piece of bread that was left on the table by depositing it in his bulky dish. Again they weren't necessary words or questions, I get up fast with fear to listen to something that I had not wanted to hear but it would have been practically impossible, his mouth was constantly full, forcing the food that entered his mouth messy to be crushed and devoured, I felt disgust, no more hunger.

I turned to the building, something should be around, I did not know what I was looking for but something would there, it was part of my faith, I wasn't alone and I was positive of it. I found a room, quite small without door or light, I got my head in to investigate, my eyes became accustomed to the black dark almost immediately, there was fresh moisture and breathing it was as a gift for my lungs, to my surprise in that small room was a shower, I stretched my hand to discover how it worked and I don't know how or what I did but the water began to fall. I got a piece of cardboard that was lying on the floor outside putting it as protection for my feet; I thought about fungi, I quickly went under the icy water enjoying it in a priceless way. I don't remember how long the shower was, it had been very comforting, I dressed the same sweat clothes that I had worn all day, it didn't matter if I was fresh and clean. I started walking back to the car to find out which would be our plan, while not expecting much communication in any case. When I jumped to skip a mud puddle I hit my head with something hard, it was a green apple hanging from a branch, enormous, as waiting for me, I felt saliva sprouting in my mouth. I cleaned the apple with my hands that still wet from the shower, it shone and I even felt guilty of attacking it with my hungry bite; bittersweet, delicious. "You are driving now, always go straight, do not get out of this road, tomorrow early we should be at Foz do Iguaçu", it was my orders or plan, as I liked to think. "Yes sir!" What else could I have said? My friend lies down in the back seat and fell asleep immediately.

The night was long, it had not been necessary to stop while my stomach was almost empty unless for the apple that I had eaten the night before and liquids I had not ingested, I figured that my body consumed more than I had. I enjoyed the dark road; I had the opportunity when it dawned to see lizards and snakes crossing the hot asphalt and a large size owl in the greatness of the night. The sun had recharged its rays with energy, were strong, bright and hot, I expected to make the same effect on my body filling it with valuable fuel needed to face a new day, my eyes burnt but I could not complain, it was what I wanted. A large sign at edge of road brought all the senses back to my body and mind as did not remember much of all the hours I had driven, I tried to recall my night but everything was very diffuse, I let the thoughts for later, I'd have time to bring my memories back. I knew that we had arrived,

"Welcome to Puerto Iguazu", prayed the notice, I felt sudden panic, I began to slow down, my instructions were very clear, we were supposed to arrive at Foz do Iguaçu, had I stayed on course? The car stopped slowly as my co-author of my mistake, the questions flowed spurting in my mind, I began to feel an uncontrollable fear and tremble. "Do not park or stop in the middle of the road!", my friend said, the voice sounded like he still asleep from the back seat, I parked in the right place and I turned off the engine, the silence was total and almost painful, now the car's engine had become my accomplice. "We are a few miles from the border, hereafter I'll drive, we will enter to Brazil by Foz do Iguaçu", his voice did not demonstrate any emotion, happiness or anger, I assumed that everything was fine, I realized that they were bordering towns and that there had not been any error on my part, I apologized to me.

There was no rest, the car and its parts were still working perfectly to follow our path immediately, my tiredness was so big but not more than my curiosity, I wanted to see everything, impregnating me of new smells and aromas, noises and squeals of the birds in the distance, new green, large and deep green, new people of different shades and colors; white, black and Asian, and evidently, everything was new to me. It took not much to set a foot on Brazilian territory, I gave my identity to a person dressed in military or police uniform, I could not differentiate, nor I knew them, time later I learned that they were military police, something new but a police again. It did not take much time with the paperwork between lines, stamps and questions to which no-one remembers having responded, I didn't understand what they were saying, they spoke in Portuguese, a language that came sweetly to my brain to stay there forever, I knew because I remember not long after having changed my habit of dreaming in Spanish by the dreams spoken and heard in Portuguese. The Brazilians were very nice, smiling most the time.

My tired eyes that morning were reluctant to any tiredness, they wanted to see and understand everything quickly, it was like one picture after another and mainly it red brightly land. My ears were acting separately, recording everything that could produce a noise or sound different from what they already knew. My sense of smell was struggling to memorize the smell of green, moisture and food. All senses had possessed my body and my mind. Between my brain and my throat I heard screaming, "Brazil!" I had achieved it while it was not the end of my way, but I had already entered into a new life.

During the trip my struggle was constant to not sleep, many times I was losing the battle but my senses took advantage of any oversights, odor or noise to wake me up, the pleasant warmth of the south of Brazil seemed more a cozy blanket to the whip of heat in northern Argentina. Waterfalls, rivers, huge plantations, zebu cattle, houses in the hills, caravans of trucks on the roads, gigantic gas stations, banana plants everywhere instead than just trees to which I was accustomed to see, lights, many lights everywhere and the smell of green followed me, no matter where I was, day and night. We crossed great and marvelous cities with a disorder that seemed very organized, modest neighboring homes next to mansions and nobody seemed to be annoying with it. "Butecos or barzinhos", small bars, were always with people with its doors or curtains open to everyone who would like to enter to drink or eat, they talked quite loud and all at once, as if everyone knew each other, they weren't arguing, they talked about soccer, mainly.

Far on the horizon I spotted a patch of light, it was night, quickly the lights began to embrace us, I felt as entering into a new world, it was the most perfect thing I had ever seen in my life, there were no corners, nothing cracking the monotony of long and perfect aligned streets and what dared to do was below or above those perfect streets, nothing was out of place, like a work of art, a painting without excesses of oleo, a drawing with the perfect hue of black graphite, nothing was left out. This city was the perfect example theory that cities grew from necessity and without organization and planning, this had been planned, made to measure. If anyone needed to go to a doctor you had to go to the medical sector where gather all together with hospitals, clinics and laboratories. To buy in any store you had to go to the commercial sector where you will find stores like Sears and others, divided into big buildings having so many floors into the sky as deep in the ground, all connected by modern mechanical stairs and so with everything, even the diplomatic sector, where all embassies are side by side and the government also with their ministries on the Esplanade and in the back end the National Congress and Itamaraty, which is the Ministry of Foreign Affairs. Amazing!, Oscar Niemeyer had created a work of art which began to be built in 1960, the biggest art work in the world, a city in the form of an aircraft, divided between South and North. Also with the time they had overpopulation problems but all was so good-planned that visionaries built satellite towns, small cities like any other in the world and with all possible disorganization, thus these satellite cities were not staining the perfect architecture as the big city and new capital of Brazil, Brasilia.

We parked in front of a building; I don't know how my friend knew which was because all for me were identical, many and all with lighted windows. He got down of the car without saying a word, I figured I had to follow him; he knocked a door and two people opened as waiting or ready to receive someone who positively was not me, so I stepped back. They greeted us very cordially, they were a couple from southern Chile, that fact made me feel more confident, and at least they spoke my language. I was introduced to them without further detail, just by my first name, what else my friend could might know about me?, they offered us a soda, which abruptly and perhaps in the wrong time and impolitely I accepted, I drank it as if it had been the last one in the world, the same with the second glass. "Are you guys hungry?", both of us answered in unison, "Yes", "No", obviously my response was the positive one, my friend quietly insisted, "No, thank you, we must go, I just came to deliver this envelope, which I think is urgent". "Stay and eat something or maybe you may want to come tomorrow for dinner", insisted. "Thank you, I'll let you know" and we left, I had no opportunity to at least ask for their names.

"Can we come tomorrow?" I asked but the answer was very clear and direct, "They are my friends", I felt four words hammering my head, one per each pronounced word and those words echoed for a long time. After a few minutes of driving we stopped at another building, much smaller, somehow dirty and with very dimmed light, I sensed the difference between the South and the North, huge difference, the aircraft of the city had been architecturally planned but also it had executive class, tourist and third.

We entered the lugubrious apartment; a living room, small, a table against the wall with a chair, a bath with a toilet and a shower that it was almost on top of the toilet, curiously made me think about the aerobic that would be necessary to take a shower and a kitchen with a stove of two sides, the kitchen sink was extremely and curiously small. I have not quite stopped looking the place when I felt the air breaking and shatter on my head with a shower of letters piled up. "You can stay here tonight, tomorrow I will be going to work at six thirty in the morning and you cannot stay here", the lights suddenly went out, I looked for the nearest wall sitting supporting my back. The night was endless, the heat was frightening, I thought in a long bath but I did not dare asking for fear to be reprimanded or expelled from the apartment, I was hungry, I felt a deep pain in the stomach and what I would do the next morning?, I asked myself again and again. I didn't have a dime; I didn't know the language, much less where I was or where to go. I wanted to pray, to ask, I wanted to cry, but I remembered that it would be a false cry, without tears, the latest I had lost them in the car crossing the mountains when I thought of my mother.

I heard him walk, take a shower, I knew he had prepared coffee because the aroma was wonderful, for a second the coffee aroma made me forget all my future problems and questions of the moment, I had never wished more than that moment a sip of that magic potion, his voice grim reaper vanished all what was in the air as if by magic, "Let's go", I took my bag and I followed him, he locked the apartment's door making sure that the door would be impenetrable. Going downstairs it came to my mind the last thing he had said, "Let's go", there was a hope, as expecting a downpour from a raindrop or perhaps a miracle from a thought. I stopped outside the passenger door of his car; my friend got in the car, ignited the vehicle's engine and ran away. Without realizing it and with his quick departure I was standing in the middle of the street, the tires made a big squeak in the asphalt driving away like he had just finished robbing a bank, the car disappeared quickly. I did not notice a car passing through that made me react with much fright, with a jump I was back to the sidewalk. No signs said welcome to Brasilia, anywhere, but there I was, I had come, perhaps I wasn't welcome nor expected any sign saying that, I would have to think about what could be my next step, a meal, for sure. My new friend did not give me the opportunity to say goodbye, I wanted to thank him for the trip, otherwise I would not be standing in the middle of the street in another city in another country and sincerely I felt it, with great pleasure I was his friend for three days, unfortunately he didn't have the same feeling, he didn't want to be my friend.

The heat becomes violent; I started to walk without direction, now I could appreciate being a little calm details of the neighborhood, very commercial with two-story buildings, business at the first level and above small apartments, perhaps the same type of the previous evening where I spent my night. I discovered that I could read and understand more than what I imagined, I needed a Spanish-Portuguese dictionary, I had enough time to study but I was also hungry and desperately wanted a shower. I spotted a pushing cart in a corner, I went there and I saw a slim man, tall with brown skin, he put to work a small gasoline engine connected to a pair of metal rollers, quite smoky and noisy machine. To my surprise he started to grind a few timbers in rolls that looked like cane, similar to what I used to cut into thin strips to make the supports for kites with the difference of these timbers, the juice came out, green, pale green juice, everything was green, even the sugar cane juice. He filled a glass of dubious cleaning and added a few drops of lemon, my curiosity grew and the cart-man realized that, "Five Cruzeiros", he said with a smile showing his large teeth, very white. "No money", I said trying to let him understand. He put his hand on my shoulder and gave me the glass, from a box in the interior of the cart he pulled a couple of pieces of ice depositing it in the glass of the green juice splashing onto the floor and into my hand. Without thinking twice and like in slow motion I started to drink it. The smell of this juice was very similar to wet wood and pleasantly sweet, as nothing before I had tested. I did not count the minutes, if they were more than seconds but all sumo was down my throat, I could hear it falling into my empty stomach as something magical. The man in the cart looked at me with his big and black eyes and eyebrows lifted in the form of a question. "Good, very good" I said. "Bom, muito bom?" He repeated in Portuguese giving a huge laugh that echoed in the empty street. He shook my hand for a long time and said many things that obviously I didn't understand, I just smiled to him and it seemed that my smile was enough pay. I started to walk again but now in the opposite direction, I was not who was going to go in the same direction, I would have been an arrogant tempting my good luck betting in the same number and the same table. It was sugar cane, I didn't know that existed sugar made from cane, in Chile is, or was, beet. I became a fan of sugar cane, many times I asked for it and it was given me, if not simply, I borrowed it, a great source of energy but not forever, it helped me for many days, as a result of this sugarcane my unconscious body was demanding something else, I needed salt. I had to rest, to sleep, to stretch my body after nearly a week of living sitting, I smelled the pestilence of my body and people looked at me strange, I had no forces or pride as to feel shame, as I not opened my mouth to say a word, neither in Spanish nor in Portuguese I went visible to all as a Brazilian indigent. A night where I had no control of my body and much less of my mind, I heard voices around me, seemed as far away, I come to think that the difference between life and death was nothing more than another dimension where the ears were losing the power to hear clearly and the voice went only as far as the esophagus. I lost consciousness.

In that state I traveled around the world, I returned to Chile, to my mother's house, I visited seas and deserts, high and low plains, I also met many people, I did not recognize anyone but everyone knew me because I was called by my name. The time of the time was a problem, I wanted to know where and when I was, what day of the week it was and what day would be the next. I didn't feel thirst or hunger, anger or compassion, I just wanted to sleep and they make me sleep until sleep became long and unconscious, almost eternal, so peaceful that I had not wanted to never be awake, I couldn't have wished it by the fear to be a sin to break that enchanted moment, I allowed them to let me carry out.

I opened my eyes as my forces allowed me, I had fear and curiosity to the intense light that was going through my eyelids, there was no pain nor consciousness again, just peace. Everyone looked at me with an angelic smile, I deeply sighed to fall back in the deepest of the dreams.

The smell of ether in the air was strong and sharply that hurts my bronchi and lungs, that smell was painfully strange, I began to cough to drown me, I wanted to open my eyes, I wanted help, I needed to see, I needed to breathe, I knew I had my eyes open but I couldn't see the most minimal hope of light. A male nurse with a forced effeminate voice plunged a needle in my arm to the bone, I screamed as I had never done it, again and again in long periods up to sob.

"How do you feel?" "I don't know", I answered. "The doctor is coming, you may ask him". There appeared a serious man. "Could you give me the name and phone number of a family member?", "I need to warn them that they may come to pick you up, you will be released from the hospital". "What happened? "Where am I?". The doctor patiently explained to me about my coma by an excess of sugar consumed, he made a detailed explanation of my vital signs, recent results of blood tests and possible consequences, I had problems with my eyes, my blurred vision confirmed what he said, he advised me to visit an eye doctor as soon as possible. He gave me several pill bottles with medicines and carefully he explained the instructions on how to take them. "Do you understand?. Do you have any questions?". "Please dress-up, here are your clothes". "No doctor, I have no questions, thank you for everything". Lightest clothing with a strange fragrance that was not mine nor acknowledged of whom, there was no place where to look for what was mine, nowhere. I went out to the street, totally lost, how much time had passed? Many carts had been outside the hospital selling fruits; bright red watermelons, sweet melons, juicy oranges and other so many that I did not know, everyone shouted their products; I could not have eaten any bite. The screaming, the laughter and the tears of children bothered me. I wanted to walk but I stopped, I turned my head to look at all the people that was around me, they spoke Portuguese and I understood them, I got closer to an old woman and I asked her where the southern zone was, she replied, I had understood and they understood me.

I walked all day without previously established direction other than to the south, it was night and I felt tiredness, hunger, and thirst. Without intention of finding something I got my hands in my pants' pockets, there were two hundred

Cruzeiros in new bills, all the same, even sharing the same smell. I went to the first open market that I found, I asked for bread, water and fruits. With the paper bag in my hands I walked until I found a bench, I sat and ate as long ago I did it. I enjoyed it. I could not speak because my mouth was constantly filled then I said mentally "Thank you". I decided to rest on the same bench that had served me as a table for my dinner and as I did a long time ago, too, I fell asleep. I rested and I once again knew what a rest was, I had no strength to dreaming or thinking, I just let myself go. I wanted to think and analyze how much had won and how much I had been lost, and if I had lost anything what it had been. Sure I knew I had won something, I felt it and had it, finally I fell asleep but not before a small leap in the bench, I just missed my small bag with my old clothes, I felt pity, I had to feel its lack, I was empty hands.

I woke up early, with much encouragement and wanting to do something, I needed to fill my free time, I needed to be someone, pay and reward the good things that had happened to me and fight for the bad to not ever return. Half of block away I found a man, perhaps fifty years old or something like that, he looked as seeking for answers, his face expressed some frustration, I got close to him asking that happened and what he needed. "The car does not work, I need to get to the church in ten minutes, I am the pastor of the church". I can't deny that I had mixed feelings; I thought a real emergency would be getting to a hospital, a job or a sick person on his deathbed. I opened the car's hood, I checked the carburetor and the points in the engine and I adjusted the distributor. "Try now", I shouted, he nervously climbed into the car turning the key in the contact and the engine began to roar. He jumped in the car as if the watch was marking the minutes before the final judgment. "Do you see that house with the tall gate?", "Yes, that", pointing to a comfortable house painted light green with dark green gate. "Come tomorrow at six o'clock in the evening, I will pay you". He didn't ask for my name neither told me his.

Six o'clock in the afternoon, before knocking the gate the pastor approached. "Please, come in. Do you know something about plumbing?", he pushed me towards the bathroom. "Do you have tools?", "The toilet does not work, it's clogged". If you finish the job before seven o'clock I would like you to go with me, I have to pay you for your yesterday and it today's job". Those words and the promise of compensation motivated me to do a good job. No, I had no tools, I decided to put my hand into the toilet, my only option, between my fingers I had food, fat and shit, a lot of shit. I let the water run several times until it flowed freely. If this would be my job, my opportunity then I should do it well, as I could and even with my fingernails I cleaned the toilet using shampoo that I found in the shower, a few minutes later the toilet shone alongside the black floor tiles. Minutes before seven o'clock I came out of the bathroom, the pastor was leaving the house, I was glad having reached him in time to receive my well deserved reward. "Oh, yes, let's go", guiding me to the door by one of my elbows, I jumped into his car and we left, minutes later we arrived at an Evangelical Church, there were no crosses or saints. The pastor greeted to all around him shaking their hands, smiling. He suddenly changed his expression just at the exact moment to confront the parishioners, he closed his previous smile looking to the high ceiling, to a fixed point, and he spoke, shouted, sang and wept at the same fixed point on the ceiling. The parishioners shouted as in a different score contorting in a violent dance. I sat in the front row, I felt privileged, and how it could be different if I came together with the pastor, all looked at me, almost with curiosity. After a few minutes he made mention of my person, the pastor did not know my name then he referred to me as the person who had fixed his car and unclogged his toilet, there was not time for surprises when everyone in the temple shouted in unison looking at me in a threatening and challenging way. "Accept God, Accept God, Accept God", over and over again. I believe I did smile, perhaps nervous. When the desperate chorus begins to lose intensity and the lamps in the temple calmed down by shaking in the air, the pastor looked at me firmly calling the attention and order to the site, he said, "God is great, forgives and pay all our debts". I understood.

I tried a couple of times to collect my money, for which I had worked, on the first attempt the pastor ignored me by closing the door and the window's curtains as soon as I approached outside his home, he did not come out in the afternoon, or at least until I left. The second and last opportunity that I tried to collect my money I did it in a more prepared way, more detailed and studied, I had a plan. I waited next to his house, without showing myself to not alert him of my presence, the pastor opened the heavy gate giving his face in front of me, no more than one inch from my nose. To my surprise he lifted his right arm as being in a fascist position and without a word regarding his debt began to recite blasphemies against me by invoking Jesus to guide me in the right direction, the correct way according to him and that road was simply that, I should continue my way without disturbing him or going back, Jesus had paid off his debts with me. As the gruesome end and for my most complete frustration, the pastor as possessed by some entity turn his eyes blank recoiling his arm high, closed the gate, door, window and curtains with his left arm. I never saw him again even I never went to walk near his house, I had learned my lesson, and thereafter I realized that I should pray for myself.

Memories always returned to me beating me in a violent way and I had trouble to catalog them and think about them, I needed to remember something positive, something that would bring me hope, value and meaning to the moment in which I was, to the moment I was living, to my plan without rhyme or reason but I was there and didn't have options again, just run my time until something happens in my life, and, with my life. My memories took me back to some ten years earlier or more, when I met through my father a client of his, Mr. Theodore, a Jew who had arrived in Chile after the second world war, he told me many things, he called me "Little Manager", he had a small business where he sold toys, mostly imported, winding type and battery operated. On some occasion in which I should collect some money for my father he made me wait a whole afternoon to what I did not seem to me fair treatment and complained to him, he smiled at me saying that I had to return the next day but to let my pride at home, my anger was so great that I couldn't understand it. My dad was furious but not with Mr. Theodore but with me, to my father I had failed in a simple task as take back home a simple check, I told him what had happened, it wasn't sufficient explanation to repair my error, he demanded me that the next day I should apologize to Mr. Theodore. It made me difficult to sleep that night; my impatience was higher than my sleep and tiredness together. After school I left again to my important task, it was a personal challenge. I went to his business again and I stared at him apologizing for my mistake of the previous day not without before telling my discomfort by being forced to apologize, even today I recognize I had not been rude with him. Mr. Theodore ignored me for a few minutes asking me to wait outside his business, again. A few minutes before closing for the day he gave me a check in a sealed envelope and without looking at me he said, "I need tomorrow Saturday you go to my house, I need to send something to your father, you are invited to have lunch with me and my wife, at twelve o'clock, do not miss it". I assumed that I should be taking money from the collection to pay for the bus ticket, as it was a check I was forced to walk nearly forty blocks back home, I came out with a lot of anger and powerlessness and only thinking about that man but almost getting home I was already thinking about that lunch, I was never before been invited by someone other than my family or relatives, I felt very important.

It was twelve o'clock sharp when I squeezed the button of the door chime on the huge carved wooden gate, a couple of minutes later appeared Mr. Theodore with a huge smile, he invited me to enter and we went directly to the dining room, lunch consisted of a dish with soup with three or four pieces of sliced hot dogs, without salt, oil or spices, the soup was just warmed. This dish was accompanied with a large glass of water. Mr. Theodore finished his dish in a couple of minutes, he left the napkin on the table looking straight at his wife thanking for the delicious soup, looked at me wondering, "Have you eaten stones soup?, "This is better!" He replied. "You must appreciate for the little you may have and never complain about what you don't have, which could be less than you think", it was one of so many comments he launched into the air during the short time I met him.

We had to sit at the patio under a beautiful sun, he rolled up his shirt's sleeves revealing a few numbers tattooed on one of his arms, he opened a book written in French and began to read. My curiosity was much stronger than my lack of social education. "Why do you read in French?", "Because I know French very well, also English,

Spanish, German and Hebrew among other languages". "Continuing knowledge does not use any space and exalts the spirit". "Why are those numbers on your arm?", I attacked. "They are part of me, to not forget who I was and who I am", he replied without removing his eyes from his book. "Can you erase them?", I asked naively. "I think yes, today's science allows everything but I've never asked, I have no concern and less need to do so. When I see them, that it is all day and every day helps me to not forget. The experience we store is nothing more than a host of mistakes, yours and mine", he said very gently. For each question I did to him I felt bombarded with his answers, I didn't understand them but I never forgot them.

About an hour later and I already with no more questions he invited me to leave. Gently took me by my shoulder carrying me toward the huge gate, he looked at me with affection, offered me his hand to shake it and told me so soft that I don't remember having noticed his strong accent, "You remember that you can cry to get what you want in life and once you get it you can laugh, not before. Good luck little manager", he dismissed me by closing the heavy gate. I don't know how much time passed and I remembered that I should take something to my father that Mr. Theodore had asked me the previous day. I squeezed the doorbell button and he opened up, "If you want you can deliver it to your father or you can keep it", closing the door forever.

Mr. Theodore died a few months later, I don't know at what age. I wanted to talk to him again, many things he said were starting to make sense in my head and I wanted to know more, I needed talk to him, I dialed his phone number, his wife answered the call, I did greet her, "I am Mauricio, it is good to talk to you again", before I could ask for Mr. Theodore she replied anticipating my next sentence, "Theodore now rests in peace, he did not suffer. He had a lot of respect for you and he remembered you fondly; I hope you remember him with the same respect and affection that Theodore felt for you". She thrilled me by her breathy voice. "Goodbye", was her last word before disconnecting the call.

Since then my memories that were huddled in my head I could organize them, I could review them, I could remember them, to exalt and practicing the wisdom of Mr. Theodore's phrases, it has served me as a guide to live in righteousness and courage facing the challenges of life. They were returning to my memory at the correct time, I learned not to complain about what I ate or little I had to eat, anything was better than a stone soup. I learned to not exalt me so easily to an adverse, I knew that would be the moment that I would have my chance to laugh but I should fight for that and much more. I learned to love and respect a person that I just met, who taught me so much.

The sun shines

I cleaned many floors and bathroom toilets, I repaired many vehicles, I babysat children, I cooked, I prepared receptions at the diplomatic level and I began to study, to learn the more I could in my spare time allowed, I visited libraries, I borrowed books, I studied and I learned languages, visiting embassies and consulates to speak with some secretaries in English, French or Italian, the Portuguese language I already mastered it perfectly. By coincidences and mistakes I was invited on several occasions to diplomatic receptions, I learned to polish me socially, to talk, to ask and to respond. I learned to eat, yes, to eat regarding how to use the silverware on the table, how to use glasses and cups of various sizes and colors. I learned how to dress and all that knowledge did not use a gram of my brain space and made me feel good. I knew when to get out of that atmosphere as soon as I saw part of the rot, there was too much drugs and obscure business, I refused to help, be part and consequently to participate, I already had everything that I had sought, knowledge of life, another life, the good life. I saw much disgrace losing everything, corrupt diplomats and irresponsible being call to return to their countries and not necessarily to be awarded or promoted from their jobs, more precisely in order to be removed. Life of luxury and crystal was that, therefore fragile as crystal, I was made of glass, polished perhaps but ultimately more resistant than the crystal. It was not difficult to enter that world and I am grateful because nor was it difficult to get out of it, I knew my limitations and one of the greatest was that I was illegally in the country, I had a tourist visa expired a few months already. The nights were all glamour and fantasy and on the day was my other reality, cleaning, a maintenance guy with up to a completely different use of language, for obvious reasons.

A day in April I read some news in an old newspaper, the Brazilian government had approved an amnesty law for foreigners who had been longer than six months in the country without criminal records. The next morning there I was, doing the line to start the process to request my legal permanence in the country. The process took a couple of months, I received a letter in the mail explaining the steps to follow but the important thing is that my application had been approved, my happiness was indescribable and I had nobody with whom to share it, I had learned to live alone, with more people but to converse with myself, to enjoy my small triumphs and lament my sad defeats. I lived in a boarding house, one bathroom for everybody and many four-bed height on certain occasions, sometimes and depending of the season could be ten or fifteen beds in each room, ten or fifteen guests sharing one bathroom in the house, hot and moist where fungi were part of the day to day, unbeaten, after showering in the morning and at night I used to put my feet in a bowl with water, vinegar and salt, it gave results but once in a while my feet itching were unbearable, I skinned with my fingers the infected parts of my feet applying any type of disinfectant that could find as a remedy. The bed belonged to me was at the very top where I had left my bag with my clothes, my towel drying stretched on the bed, the bottles with vinegar and disinfectant, another with salt and the plastic bowl on top of everything; I slept on top of bedding, I didn't want to know what kind of bugs had been among the sheets, I didn't like it but I could do nothing, I should live with that situation, it would not be forever, today I would cry and tomorrow I could laugh, being able to close one more cycle of my life, I accepted it reluctantly but was always better and safer to sleep under a roof, and it was very cheap.

Once with my Brazilian documentation in hand I decided to change the environment and new air, it was the beginning of something new, I had been able to gather some money, I bought new clothes; blue-jeans, T-shirts, underwear and sneakers and a new bag among other things, I got all my old clothes into my old bag and burned it, I could have given away everything but I decided to make this a ritual. I wanted to also burn my memories of that boarding house together with the fungi, lice and fleas, no, I couldn't, I wanted to keep the memories, It would be very helpful in case of the need of those memories, I would have never been able to erase them from my mind, inadvertently I learned that these memories are our tattoos that will stay forever in our brain and soul, beautiful or ugly, good or bad, they always will be our memories, a part of our lives, perhaps simpler and lighter is to carry a tattoo on the arm than at heart, perhaps hurts less.

With my new bag full of my new clothes I arrived to a hotel on the opposite side of the bus terminal, I had left the boardroom forever. That night at the hotel I opened the bed linens, sheets were white and it smelled bleach and detergent, I went to the bathroom to take a long shower watching me in white tiles on the walls, my image was fuzzy but I could distinguish and feel my smile, naked as I had not been in a long time I snuggle in this huge bed not wanting to sleep, I wanted to enjoy that moment, make it eternal, and if I fall asleep I wanted to wake up every minute to enjoy the smell of cleaning. A little made me so happy.

When the phone rang informing me that I should wake up I was already awake, it was six o'clock in the morning, my bus to Sao Paulo would not leave until ten o'clock in the morning, I took a shower again and went back to my bed, which I felt mine. I dressed by nine o'clock and with much sadness I left the room with direction to the bus terminal, I ate something and I boarded the bus to my new destination, I was nervous and impatient, I thought my life changed, my life was taking a turn in one hundred eighty degrees. More than six hundred miles of travel that we did in nearly eighteen hours, everything was new; green aromas, wonderful waterfalls, colorful and sweet fruits and new people. We went out of the jungle to enter gigantic cities and we came back to deep into the jungle, torrential rains in which the driver of the bus had to decrease the speed to almost nothing to be able to see the road, heat, high heat that transformed the rain into steam in a matter of minutes and where to see also became complicated. Thousands or millions of insects of all sizes and shapes painted the windshield of the bus spreading blood and yellow substances in a harmonious collective suicide, just missing the music to simulate a work of art prepared instead of a tragedy of nature.

We finally entered in Sao Paulo; nearly two hours took the journey from the first lights of the city to slowly come to the old bus station, "Estação Da Luz". An impressive multicolor acrylic roof, all colors were there, I could sense the joy of the city and its habitants in every detail. There was no comparison with Brasilia, this was a much older and even more dirty city, street vendors offered fruits, foods and juices by discarding the raw material of their products to the street directly, flies and giant cockroaches flying in search of more trash, but the smile on the faces of people compensate for the dirt, it seemed another country within the same. I had the address of a hotel that had been recommended to me, clean and cheap they told me, I walked around the bus terminal to be able to locate me, a couple of taxi drivers approached me offering their services, I asked them how much they charged me to take me to the hotel, I showed them the address, the first driver told me that he could not go, it was very far and the second driver said he could do it without before demanding payment for the trip back to the terminal because he might not find passengers back to downtown, we reached an agreement on the price, it was much more than what I had budgeted but the taxi driver offered me do mediate between the hotel's owner and my stay, it would be cheaper than the normal price, he said. I accepted, I didn't have many options. We traveled in the taxi for more than half of an hour between dark streets and illuminated and wide avenues to reach the door of the hotel, the taxi driver helped me with my bag and left me in front of the wide countertop, he recommended me with the receptionist telling him I was his friend, the discount of the price for the room was considerable, I was very happy, the taxi driver wished me good luck, I paid him as agreed and went off showing a wide smile of gratitude.

Obviously I proceeded with my new ritual, a long shower and clean bed, I was surrendered by tiredness, I didn't enjoy or relax that time, and I fell asleep immediately. I woke up by the noise of vehicles on the street, it was already hot, it was more than nine o'clock in the morning, I was on the fourth floor, I opened the curtains of the window of my room to see a sea of vehicles and a multicolored roof below, identical to which I had seen the night before at the bus terminal, incredibly identical, the same colors covered by triangular shapes, entering and coming out buses also, I ran to the opposite window and my eyes met with a big sign saying, "Estação Da Luz". I laughed out loud, impossible not to do.

In the next two days I dedicate myself to find where to live, I knew nothing and nobody but I took it with patience and maturity, there were dozens or hundreds of small cities, hundreds or thousands of neighborhoods to choose, which was better than the other or worse, I wanted somewhere where I could find work near where I live, I visited many places, I spoke with many people and each of these people had their personal experience and opinion of what to do or where to live and work. Go to the ABC's region and you can work in any automaker, no, said another, live near downtown and work in a bank, ignore it, live on the north side, there are many new industries, said others. The truth is that for the place where I could go were industries and banks, hotels and homes and many rooms for rent. I ride the subway and get off at a station, any, it was Vila Mariana, I walked a couple of blocks to a stop against a signboard that said was a room for rent, I knocked the door asking to see the room, it was on the ground floor near the lateral entrance of the house, it had a bed, a night table and a small shelf for hanging clothes. I asked the homeowners about the rent but in exchange for an answer they read me the conditions, "This is a family home, parties and visitors out of day time are not allowed. We require cleaning and organization". What else I could ask for? It was perfect, I would have tranquility and privacy, I accepted immediately paying in advance. I went back to the hotel to pick up my belongings stopping at a department store to buy bed liners, sheets mainly and towels. The bathroom was shared with two other people but it was clean, my neighbors' room came also to speak with me to communicate their rules with respect to the care of the bath to prevent fungi, mainly, the only important direction was to shower with sandals, so I went immediately to buy a pair of plastic sandals for the shower. Everything was already engaged, prepared and accommodated; the next step would be to find work.

After a week I was accepted as a bank assistant, I never knew to what or who I have to assist but it didn't matter, my job consisted in organizing and summing checks so I did with much desire and pleasure, I enjoyed it completely and felt more eager to do it when every two weeks I received my pay, it was a fair, clean money and which filled me with pride. I spent almost a year doing this same work, monotonous but not to the point of getting tired because my salary already had increased four times, two due to inflation and other twice for the good work I had done plus my punctuality and dedication and some other ideas I gave to improve the process. A day the branch manager called me to have a conversation with him, obviously I worried, and he asked me to stay after working hours. He was direct, "I am being promoted to the post of Vice-president within our headquarters", he told me that it would require many sacrifices, relocating, family adaptation and more but he was willing to take all the risks because this was the opportunity of a lifetime, which he had been waiting for twenty-two years. I was very happy for him and I told it to him, I was very honest but I didn't understand why he told me such important and personal news, I dared not to ask him directly why me, I thought if he wouldn't have anyone else with whom to share this great news but I left him to continue talking. "I want you to be the next branch manager, you have the skills and abilities therefore I would like to send you to Manaus to do the course", obviously I was surprised, I was being rewarded for something I had done well and the most important thing for me was that someone recognized it without I even ask for it. The manager asked me to take my time to think about it. Was hard to fall asleep that night, having nothing in my hands yet I felt a winner. I thought how far I could get in life thanks to my own efforts, I was still very young and thought of the rest of my co-workers, why none of them had been chosen over me?, many of whom had spent years working for the same bank, the same agency and I could say, all of them with much sacrifice and dedication also. What would they think when knew about my ascent and rapid promotion? Of course I would accept it, I had no doubt, it was what I wanted and life offered it to me without anything in return.

I arrived early at my workplace, just the guard was there, I turned on the lights and I started doing my daily routine, sort checks, add them and confer the sum, separating checks of larger amounts to confer the signature of the holder so I spent the morning, each of my co-workers were concentrated in their own work, I needed to look at the face of each of my colleagues. "Could anyone know?", I wanted to share, I needed to share that tremendous news that was turning into my mouth as if it was a chew gum without flavor in need to be spit out, it was hurting me but every time I intended to open my mouth, I stopped, I should keep the secret.

The truth is I didn't like to share some of my life with someone, nor had that someone, I had no friends and I talked with very few people, I had a habit to not trust, I should have to talk about my family, why I was alone there and so far from home, it was not normal to say the least. I enjoyed reading and learning every day about everything, I could absorb much information easily. I spent most weekends doing my laundry, ironing and organizing my room, I walked a lot, I visited museums, I liked to window shop, although I hardly bought anything, I wasn't becoming a stingy but I couldn't conceive in my head spend on buying something to let it saved somewhere. Typically on weekends I had good lunches, long and slowly, I could spend hours sitting in front of a table tasting Brazilian delicacies but yes, I felt alone. I missed my family, my neighbors, people but not their problems and dramas, I had already enough of all that.

That year living in Sao Paulo I met a young woman, more or less my age or maybe a little younger than I, I called her "friend", I felt it, she was the person closest to me, we went out to walk, to talk and often eat anything. In a certain occasion this friend invited me for dinner at her house to introduce me to his family, I found out that she lived far away, perhaps more than one hour away by bus, it was a very simple and poor house, her parents were dressed as someone coming back from working in the field, peasants, with dirty hands, creased and battered with dried mud, serious faces, emotionless, they didn't transmit sadness or joy. The only person who smiled and talked about anything was my friend, appeared on the table two small glasses with cachaça, a strong liquor, a sugar cane distillate, the man took a sip without producing a notch, as if it had been water, I wanted to do the same but I choked and coughed until tears sprang to my eyes, I badly could breathe, my throat had closed. "So, you are who want to marry my daughter". That phrase, that question seemed more an assertion and confirmation that left me frozen, perspiration began to sprout on my forehead, I have not recovered yet from the strong drink of almost pure alcohol and plus the surprise of my future marriage. "Where is the bathroom?", I continued coughing and it was the only thing I could say. That environment weighed too much, the air also, it was dense, "Outside, to the right", she said directing me to the bathroom, it seemed an eternity to walk up to the door. I didn't see the bathroom; I kept walking quickly until I realized I was already running. I disappear, literally, I spent four hours to get back to my room, and I took the wrong bus because I climbed the first bus I found. I wanted a friend, not a wife.

"How one finds a friend?" I thought; with no obligations or responsibilities, perhaps my destiny was not to have a friend. I needed to share, talk, laugh and to cry with someone, I wanted someone to hear me, someone to laugh with about my follies and stories of every day, an arm where to support me, when nostalgia was attacking me, someone to tell me that I was wrong or correct when I made a life's plan, of being criticized as also congratulated by some achievement. I knew many people but none of them met those conditions fully, I thought. "Why everything in life is so difficult?" I thought screaming it to me. The sadness began to persecute me and I was impregnating of it like a bad smell.

How wrong I was, life is for that, to learn and we can only do it through our mistakes, to have a friend is to be one first, without obligations and responsibilities it is impossible, that's all you need, to start; the obligation to respect and to be respected, the obligation to be faithful and loyal, the obligation of trust and be trusted, the responsibility of caring for a friend and his or her friendship and more, the love we must give towards a friend. The fact of hanging a sign around our neck saying, "I wanted a friend" is not sufficient or saying "I am a good friend" is so false that neither self believes it, just one person may assert such predicament, your own friend, we should know and learn how to give, not excessively but with the quality and just life and time teach it. I've had very few friends in my life and sometimes I felt I betrayed them, I never again contacted them and I let those feelings vanished, they were good friends, I am in debt.

After three days without news from the branch manager, or former manager he showed up saying, "Sorry, really", he said looking at me with sadness as a sympathizer. I didn't clearly understand but I knew something was not going well at all. The chosen had been another, not me. He wanted to explain to me with more details what had happened but in return he offered me another job as a consolation prize, the salary would be the same and inclusive I would be entitled to stay in the same small desk and chair allocated to me over a year ago. Because my wounded pride and abuse I did not accept his offer, I gave him thirty days notice to leave my position with the bank, I would find another job, I was already determined, I considered it a mockery even though very honest that he seems. Many were the letters that I received through the internal mail from the bank of different managers requesting me to reconsider my stay, even the visit of a Vice-president of the bank appeared one morning, they would send me anyway to Manaus to study and be a sub-manager. My answer remained the same, no. I wanted to fight for the Grand Prize, he finally told me direct and clear. "Nobody will respect you, you are too young", sentenced. I had not thought of it that way and basically he was right but the pain and the disappointment of the situation weren't away very easily. The time made me accept it although years later I would lose a couple more of these managerial offers for the same reason.

I look back thinking, how much I would give of my life to have the same answer today.

It was very easy to find a new job, now I was a price negotiator to deal with the automakers industry, I was hired to prepare by hand intricate analysis and costs' maps, raw materials and labor for auto parts industry. I did that work for nearly fifteen years, for different companies and products.

The return

It was time to relax and think of vacations, I would visit my family in Chile; it had been two long years. The return journey was slow, full of memories. Many things had changed in two years, me, physically, I perceived it, mentally were others that found me more mature, more man, as they said proud of me, a bit stranger seemed to me that kind of comments when they never cared about me and they were people I knew very little. "This is your cousin, say hi to him", "How is working in Brazil, I thought of going there too", "I have prayed a lot for you", "Come and spend a few days with us so we can talk", "Can you give me your address in Brazil, a telephone number?". I took my mother's hand rescuing us, we got to walk without direction, and I hugged her and I knew how much I missed her and how much I love her and how much I needed her when I was away. I thought I found her more mature, she was not happy but had accustomed to her life, to her unhappiness, "People get used to", mom said, because you get tired walk weeping by the corners of the house.

My brother had grown taller, too, my sister was pregnant, she had left college to take care of her pregnancy and also of her man, she heated water for his shower, he did not like to bathe with cold water, he was abusive, fortunately for my sister and my mother that marriage was very short, my singular brother-in-law ended up dying after a robbery he had committed. I didn't want to know more details, the issue had become a drama, some defended him and others attacked him. A beautiful girl was born bringing the joy back home, my mother lived mostly for her granddaughter, she sewed and knit for her, mom constantly got out the house to buy fruits and vegetables for the baby, she took care of both, her daughter and granddaughter. What at first I considered the biggest mistake of my sister the situation became a solution for many people, my sister should be mother and father to her daughter, life would charge her with sacrifices but when sacrifices are made with love, there is no pain, my sister told me. My mother found a sense to continue living, she was transformed into a person who I didn't know, she opened the windows of the house, left to enter the pure breeze and the sun, also to her life. My younger brother was another story, between the new complicity between my mother and my sister my brother didn't have room, I tried unsuccessfully many times to thread a conversation with him, he accused me of leaving him alone, having abandoned, he felt jealous of my new niece and hatred towards my father. Time, the beatings and the years made him to mature, ended happily married and father of three daughters, he could never overcome the sickly hatred towards my father, and we never talked about it, still hurting him.

She had a fabulous body, a sweet smile, a black hair as the night, legs almost turned by hand protected by expensive panties of nylon, fine shoes with high heels, we look each other, we like each other too, it was like an electric shock sent from heaven, I wanted to think that yes, that Cupid existed and how not, if there I was, wounded by love. "Could I invite you to watch a movie?". She accepted immediately. A little more than a month later we were married. We ended living in Brazil; I left first and my brand new wife with our daughter nearly six months later.

Each day that passed my life begun to make sense, I had many reasons why to fight, new emotions were born every day and I didn't even know from where, from my brain, my soul, my heart?, I didn't know how to explain it myself but I knew I had to live through them. I worked hard and lived life with passion, came into my life everything I had missed, I didn't feel the lack of anything or anyone from my past, I could finally say that I was happy, we were incredibly happy. It wasn't a love necessarily inherited from fathers to sons or brother to brother, it was like watching to birth flowers, with varied perfumes of peace and love. I knew it, I was deeply in love and children began to water this garden as they came to life to see more flowers grow, my life had been transformed into a garden, in a jungle of flowers.

A few years later we already were a family, social and morally formed, we were five. We had a big two-story house, a big yard, my wife was in charge of filling it with flowers and exotic plants, we were filling the house with new furniture as the family grew, we bought our first car, an old Volkswagen beetle but very well preserved as I liked to say, perhaps I justified saying it to excuse it's years of activity through the streets but the important thing was not the car itself but the joy of getting up in the car us five for a weekend trip, or to the Zoo, to the safari, to the squares and parks and wherever we wanted to. Many times the emotion overwhelmed me when we arrived home, already at night usually, we parked the car, carrying the remains of lunch or any food that would have left over and toys, baby bottles half-filled, bags with diapers and finally loading the tired and sleeping creatures one by one to their beds, I even compared those images with drawings of angels to see them as healthy, happy and innocent, I wanted more children to what my wife refused, "Three are enough", she said to me, "You have to think about the future". Her concern was always about the future, "Would be our modest financial situation enough to feed five mouths?", "What if a day we need more money?", "Wasn't it better to ensure a good future for three children to feed and educate than raise more children half way?" Obviously she was absolutely correct and I was forced to accept the facts of responsible parenthood. I thought that small children running behind me would be forever, I didn't want to think they would grow and also I would be old. "Why I should stop and think about that?" No reason, I lived those years fully.

Quickly passed the time, perhaps because they were good years, happy, without big surprises, health or financial but when the children grow up they ask for more, not literally asking but there is a school, uniforms, clothing, shoes, birthday, a safer and larger vehicle, finally, that's where the money is short, always it needed a little more of what we have or make as payroll. A new idea came to me, sell automotive parts in my country, the currency exchange and prices for the Brazilian market were favorable at that time, obviously I hadn't the economic means to prepare a large-scale commercial adventure so I decided to travel between Brazil and Chile by ground taking small amounts of auto parts, after three days of travel I delivered the parts to buyers and normally with the resulting of profit from these transactions I bought gold in Chile to be sold in Brazil. Perfect business and clean, all legal. We noticed quickly the financial difference in our lives. What could go wrong? Of course nothing.

I was preparing the second or third trip, I don't remember very clearly those details, I think it was every thirty days I had planned on making these trips, it was enough time to receive the orders of people interested in different products, buy the products and sell the gold and wait for the economic results of these two countries, being attentive to the evolution of the exchange rate, all these procedures demanded time, dedication and research and everything I knew how to do it very well. Illusions and the plans grew every day, we were already talking about imports and exports at one higher level, we would need an office, something more formal and professional than a place in our dining room, a phone and a fax line, a mailing address, at the end, everything was going well, in the right direction.

Everything was ready, I bought the products needed, I checked the car once more because it had something not working correctly with the engine, I hesitated until the last minute that I could make the trip in that car, I seek a mechanic's advise considering that I understand very well the mechanical part, nothing was found defective. I have never been superstitious, not to the point of thinking that the problems I was having with the car was a word of caution, several people told me about it, they mentioned to me, I did ignore all comments.

A few days before the trip a friend with her young daughter asked me if they could travel to Chile with us, they should be there to perform certain legal formalities, also offered me take care of one of my children during the trip, the middle one, if I thought of taking him, I hadn't thought about it but the idea did not displease me so I talked to my wife. Evidently she says no, a flat no was her answer but friends convinced her that our son could go with me, I promised to be careful and responsible and communicating constantly. There had been nothing in the world that I could refuse to her and we finished our plans.

We left at mid-afternoon, my son, our friend with her daughter, my co-pilot and I, as the car moved away I remembered seeing my wife's tears, like any mother, with a tight heart, dwarfed and scared of letting one of her babies run so risky adventure. She was calm when I promised her that I would care and protect our son with my own life if necessary. The car did not stop giving sporadic problems all the way, as soon as we arrived in Santiago everything seemed normal, exact half of our goal was fulfilled for my peace of mind and my wife's.

A week later we were already setting the return to Brazil; everything had been within expectations and with new plans to return almost immediately in a new trip. The Los Andes' mountain refused us the easy pass, dozens of problems with the car again, we took twice the estimated time to reach the Los Libertadores pass, up in the mountains. More than ten hours of twisting each one of the twenty-eight curves to reach the expected seventeen thousand feet high. We arrived extremely tired, altered nervous system, it seemed like we did all the force rather than the car's engine. I drove all day until the engine refused to continue working, we rested, I decided to put my hands in the guts of the car, between belts, hoses, cables, grease, dirt and oil and finally I found the problem, it did not properly distributed the high voltage to all the spark plugs in the same amount. Such was the joy of having been able to solve the problem that

I didn't think even in washing my hands and less in resting, I wanted the car to continue its way to the north, advance until when I order it to stop. It seemed so far-fetched to believe that much trouble would have been because just a wire, to put it in a simple way that basically the problem was a little bit more technical. My co-pilot drove, sang and even screaming of joy, the heat forced us to drive with rolled down windows, it didn't matter the mosquitoes attacking us.

I slept without perceiving where or when but not before taking a look at all in the car as to confirm that everything was and would be good, everybody singing, happy, my son looked at me in a wise way, said nothing, and just smiled almost with malice. I let me take by my tiredness letting it to embrace me, perhaps I slept for hours, and it didn't matter if we were going home, safe, except despite several hours of delay.

I opened my eyes because of the calm, the lack of noise, I was alone sitting in the passenger seat, it was already night and nobody was there, I felt cold, for a moment I thought it was from the ice of the mountains but it was impossible, we were far from there and at almost sea level, I quickly recomposed to understand what was happening,

I found my glasses, put them on me and tried to visualize. Everyone played and ran around an old gas station in the middle of nowhere, no vehicles around much less people, I started walking toward my people, "What happened?", "Why are we here?", "Why we are not moving?", I asked with my hands in height, gesturing, everyone looked at me, my co-pilot began to walk towards me, "I am sorry", the car stopped, again, I did not want to wake you up", I felt anger, disappointment, impatience, I looked at the sky, it was blue almost black and the stars glittered more than ever, there was no answer, only questions in the dark eternity.

I walked slowly without direction as waiting for an answer, "What to do now?" Thousand times I repeated it. I didn't have options again, I was half-way, the only option was to go ahead but "How?", "In what?", I felt tied hands, I looked toward inside of the car, glasses were breaded by respiration of all and everyone slept, maybe it was good, I'd have more time to be alone to find out a solution, I needed to think and expect a miracle. The night came with force; I felt the cold of the Argentinean prairie where the sun becomes treacherous overnight and freezes. I began to feel pain in my fingers, it was a notice that I should put me into action; the cold was doing its job. I opened the hood of the car and again started to stick my cold hands within the same guts which I had already previously violated in search of an answer, I only had a flashlight with exhausted batteries, I didn't have the option of waiting for the sun early in the morning to laugh at me, I would make a deal with the moon and I would explain to the sun someday of my betrayal. Hours later I had some disassembled parts and other eviscerated, I could not move the alternator's shaft with my hand, like a doctor I had found the problem and it became as simple as knowing the problem, the solution would be a consequence. The alternator bearings were overheated by eliminating all traces of lubricant allowing these to almost melt. I had the problem, the solution but not the new parts, the bearings, I waited for the day to clear, I did stop a truck driver and explained my drama, he offered me to take me to the next town, it was about six miles from there without exempting himself from guilt in the case that I wouldn't find anything in that almost ghost town. It was not greater than two blocks long by one wide, no one in the streets or a place for someone to buy something; it was so small that neither deserved the name of "village". While I walked I imagined that I was in the middle of a story where something or someone had put in the middle of the night three dusty streets and some houses, nothing else. I wanted to go back but I didn't know how, in a matter of seconds I lost my compass, I did so many laps in the same center as looking for an answer and a smile called my attention, he didn't say anything, I just walked towards him, a man who would not let me guess his age or name. I quickly remembered my mission when I tempted to open my mouth, he said, "Oh, yes, follow me, come with me. Let's see if I can help you". He pushed a door leaving it opened so I follow him, the light came suddenly and everything was illuminated, a white light, very natural, he searched on some drawers, his eyes sparkled. "Maybe in this other", whispered. He gave a cheerful laugh, stretched out his hand and gave me two small butter paper envelopes, rancid lubricant due to the passage of the years. My tiredness was so big that everything seemed distant; I wanted to get back to the car, to my people as soon as possible.

The old man and I went to the side of the road, he moved his hands to stop a truck, he opened the door and I climbed. I looked back; I saw the smile go away until his body dissipated in the dust of the road. "Did you find what you were looking for?", "What a coincidence to be me again to take you back", I gave a surprise jump in my seat, what a coincidence; he was the same man who had earlier led me to town. "Life has its mysteries", he tried to explain. It didn't take too long the trip back to the car, I jumped off the truck thanking him for the ride; I thought to have seen that smile before, later I would make memory. I walked a few steps and I turned my body to raise my hand in a gesture of appreciation, he already had gone, was not there the trucker or the truck, he had returned by the same route since I didn't see it go ahead of me.

All still sleeping, in a matter of minutes I put together the pieces and everything would be back to normal. "Push, all push, let's go!" I screamed when I was ready. As if they had been waiting for my shout all left the car and began to move the vehicle, in a jump I sat in front the steering wheel, and I remember having looked in the rearview mirror, all laughed, we were all happy and on our way home again.

Finally the engine roared again and despite my tiredness I decided to drive, I didn't much believe in superstitions, but every time my co-pilot drove something happened with the car, I thought it was only because of the way in which I drove, careful and conscious, just that. Once all accommodated to continue our journey I remembered the almost intangible experience of a few hours earlier, abruptly I noticed not having paid any money for the new bearings, I went back, the little town was just a few miles and no more than ten minutes of travel, I felt ashamed by my misconduct but I would emphasize in explaining my forgetfulness to the kind character. We had to go back to our original route; I never found the little village, and its entry of dust or its three streets. It was forever engraved in my memory the face of the old man and his smile just like the trucker's smile, they were the same.

The night came, everything worked like a Swiss watch, in about twenty hours we should be entering to Sao Paulo then be sleeping in our beds and laugh our bad luck with the car, it would be part of the past.

We entered a city, the road cut it through the middle, silent and wet, I felt the sticky air, stopped the car turning off the engine in the middle of the block. I got off, I opened the hood to check the oil and water levels, everything was normal. "What we will do now?", my co-pilot asked, I explained that we should gain time to continue driving, we had already lost many hours with the breakdowns, I was still very tired, I had almost a whole day without sleep and my co-pilot was fine and fresh, he had slept quite during the night and day so I explained to him the direction to follow, we settled again, I reclined my seat with the intention to rest and sleep. He inserted the key into the ignition and again the engine didn't work, I knew immediately, I just looked at his face that almost disfigured, between shame and sorrow, his black eyes showed by changing his skin to a bright white color, he palled without being able to express any word, his hand without control turned the key over and over again as waiting for a miracle without removing his eyes off me. I put my hand over his to stop turning the key, I could not pronounce a word, I only yelled to look out the window on my side with a sharp exhalation, searching for an answer. Just in front where we had stopped, crossed street was a mechanical workshop, I walked hitting the metal door, it opened almost immediately, a man with oil stains on his clothes, skin and hair looked at me with surprise and curiosity. "Can I help you?", he asked, I explained in a few words the problem also summarizing the details of our difficult adventure. Kindly shut the side door to open the double gate, we pushed the car with the help of two other people that worked for him until it was in the middle of a mechanic's well. The three men went to work, lights up and below, instruments connected to different parts of the engine, nobody said anything, just looks between them and occasionally towards me, it gave me the idea of a patient lying on a stretcher in any emergency room.

After half an hour waiting and looks with a certain honesty that I did not expect he said, "Here is nothing wrong, everything works, or should work without problems". "But, and the alternator?", I asked like forcing an answer or protesting to find something wrong with the engine. "Nothing", he concluded. The mechanic sat against the steering wheel, turned the key and the engine worked. "I don't know what to say, don't get me wrong, I make my money honestly and I won't even charge you because there is nothing wrong with your car", he replied with an air of sadness. "I will pay you but please find the problem", I said almost begging. "Pray, ask God to guide you and help you, He knows why he does things", he said shaking his hand against mine. It seemed a good idea and I was more convinced when he refused to accept the money that I was offering him for his services. After a strip tug-of-war got to accept the money, his eyes showed sadness.

I helped one by one of my passengers to get up and sit in the car, I felt guilty and irresponsible for all inconveniences during the return trip, the initial travel's problems were almost an anecdote compared with this. Finally my son ran into my arms, he squeezed me, kissed me as he had never done it before, "And this kiss is for mom, tell her I love her". I felt tears running down my cheeks, I wanted to answer him, and I wanted to explain that he could say it to mom the next day when coming home. "Thank you, thank you for everything dad", he said sealing any possible answer with a kiss on my mouth. Tiredness was not only mine, already about two blocks away I saw that our three passengers in the back seat fall to sleep deeply, I asked my co-pilot how he felt, if he wanted to be replaced at the steering wheel to which he answered negatively. We were a couple of hours of travel from the Argentinean-Brazilian border, it was everything I wanted, to cross the border and make me feel at home, I knew from my own experience that the Brazilian roads were better, wider and well maintained.

I accommodated on my seat, turning my body towards the window; I had something outstanding to do; talk with God. I closed my eyes and I slept.

The dream, the nightmare

Lights spun, my head came and went with an uncontrolled force, the noise of the tires against the pavement was deafening. "Let it go, release it, you will kill us!", shouted desperately my co-pilot, I opened my eyes, my heart seemed to want to jump out through my mouth, I couldn't breathe not less talk. My co-pilot of a flip released my hand from the steering wheel braking aggressively. "We crashed!", I shouted incessantly and uncontrollably. "No, it was only a dream, a nightmare; it must be because you are very tired". We were in the middle of a bridge, I sat like a spring to confirm if it had been a bad dream, I wanted to get out of the car, and I needed to recover. "I'll drive, let me drive!", I demanded. "Okay, but let me take the car to the exit of the bridge, it is very narrow and dangerous place", I agreed nodding my head. I leaned back in my seat, I needed to recuperate, I needed to calm down my heart and my breathing, as well as my senses, I didn't know what time it was but everything outside was dark. I saw the output of the bridge, it was very close and again I lost my conscience.

My head was spinning again, I felt a very strong knock at the back of my head, again lights spun incessantly around me and the tires squeal against the pavement but now with a smell very strange, a warm smell of rubber and blood. Minutes, seconds or fractions of seconds, I don't know, it seemed an eternity and from one moment to another everything was calm, just the smell was still in the air. Blindly I opened the door on my side, I looked around me and there was nothing, I could not distinguish between night and horror, slowly the images began to appear, my co-pilot had one of his feet caught between the brake and clutch pedals and his body lay folded through the window, his face in parallel with the black pavement, unconscious. My friend was tight at the height of her shoulders between the crushed metal, seemed asleep, her daughter sitting next to her mother, crying, scared, her tears and the light made a dramatic face of terror and my son wasn't there, I began to scream his name, some people ran to see the horrific scene, all ran, I was still shouting his name then I realized that my voice was silent, more I screamed less I heard my own voice, unable to speak and everyone asked me something, I could not hear or I did not understand what they asked me, I don't know, I don't remember. "Here is a boy!" Someone yelled. He was lying at the edge of the road, on the shoulder, he seemed sleeping peacefully, I took him in my arms, and he released a moan. "Let's go to the hospital, quick, fast, there is no time to wait for the ambulance!", people shouted, they guided us to a pickup, maybe a truck, everything was fuzzy and I began to think, to understand that something serious had happened. My son complained on the way to the hospital, I talked to him and told him that everything was going to be fine but please, for the love of God, the same God who I had not prayed the night before by having fallen asleep, cry, scream and cry how much he would, that I would leave him to make a scandal, if he wanted to.

We went to the emergency room, by then my son was crying of pain, I was sure because I knew very well his weeping as his siblings. They took my son from my arms to a small room where I could hear him and he was crying intensely giving me peace of mind. "We are suturing, he has a small cut on the head, just are a couple stitches", said the nurse. He began to fall asleep; his crying became like a sigh intermittent until falling asleep. I sang to him from my seat, I told him my plans, we would head home soon, we would take a bus or an airplane, whatever, I would take care of him, of his head, don't worry my son, there wouldn't be any scar or perhaps he wanted to keep it, whatever he wanted.

A man in white showed up, looked at me from the top of my head to the tip of my feet, slowly saying, "Take the drunk out of here", that was me, I looked to myself slowly than that man had looked me, I checked my black jacket, it was stained with dirt, oil and blood, a mixture that I had never seen or thought about seeing someday. "He is a family member of the child", said another nurse looking at me with pity. I was pushed to an emergency room where my son was, I didn't see him coming out of the first room, and I didn't see when they moved him of the place. My son had a tube that was coming in or out of his mouth, he was deeply sleeping. The same man in white looking the instruments said, "This very serious, he was hit in the head, I do not think he will survive", "No!", I said, it cannot be possible, he is just sleeping, "Don't you see him?", my words rumbled in my head but my mouth ignored what my head was thinking. "We'll move him to a hospital with more resources; we need to do a brain scan". I woke up in a room, alone and naked, I looked at everything without understanding, as I could I get up, I walked to the wall, it had a mirror, dirty, full of fingerprints then I saw me, I cannot say I recognized myself, in the mirror was an old man bloodstained, with his eyes swollen with a gigantic attached head from the right temple down to the neck, an eye half closed or half opened, a crooked mouth trying to follow the line of the eye, even the pain was reflected in the mirror, I was dizzy and no longer saw double but triple. As I could I found part of my clothes, trying to focus on closing one eye, see two things of the same was better than seeing three. I was almost dressed when the same man in white entered the room; he kindly snatched from my hands my shirt and my dirty jacket helping me to get dressed in logical order. "You have a cranial brain trauma, your brain suffered damage, you need to rest", he was finishing his explanation when I started to vomit, the doctor puts a garbage can in front of me, probably to don't get dirty everything and walked away. I cleaned me as I could and I came out of the room, there was nobody who I could recognize. "Are you the father of the injured child?", asked a stranger, I nodded my head with much sacrifice due to pain. "Come with me, your son was moved to Concordia, the young woman who came with you in the car needs to see you, her daughter is playing with other children and your friend waits for you in my car". It seemed that everything was under control but I could not understand everything, or nothing, I just wanted to see somebody, some well-known face. "Are you fine?", my co-pilot said, "You are alive!", I got to say despite my problems to talk. I embraced him and we cried at length, I wanted to tell him about my son but he surprised me, "I know it all. First we go to the hospital, to the nuns' hospital, we will ask to discharge your friend, she just suffered some contusions on her back, her daughter did not suffer even a scratch and then we go to Concordia to take care of your son". "And you?, I saw you dead", I insisted. The doctor gave me some medicines; we went to a hotel to take a bath and talk. The feeling I had was strange, as if it had been numbed mouth, it was hard for me to move my lips but I could communicate with choppy phrases and appealing to people guess my thoughts. We arrived at night at the hospital; they did not let me see my son, "Maybe tomorrow", was the emphatic answer. A thin man with a thick beard was waiting for me, I didn't know him, I had never seen him before but he talked me and treated me as if I was his friend from long before, "You guys need a hot soup, mate tea and some aspirin to be able to sleep peacefully". I tried to explain to him that it should stay there; my son was there and didn't know in what state. Why no one understood me? And why everyone wanted to do what they wanted? At the end I gave up and I let them take me wherever they wanted, to fight against them was the same thing that fights against me. They offered me mate tea, tea and coffee, water, soda and everything they could, I just accepted a glass of brandy, it burnt my throat and my stomach, the guts and my consciousness, within a few minutes I could discern by myself, I asked them to take me back to the hospital and so they did. I got late at night talking with a doctor in charge of unit intensive care, she explained to me that my son was with a very large brain damage, they were doing their best to reduce the swelling of the brain asking me to pray, "If he survives or God decides to leave him on this earth, his future would be uncertain, he might be a vegetable. He is in a coma". Those words nailed hard in my heart through my soul. I was sitting all night near the door to the intensive care unit and my heart was fired each time I saw people run when entering or leaving that cold room. When someone entered or left the ICU smiled me, I was watching them waiting for a response, a comment to tell me, "Your child wants to talk to you or your child wants to see you", all in vain. Nothing had changed in the morning, I asked to see him again, I cried, I begged and I pleaded, they were adamant and I was still asking for a miracle, I was extremely positive that everything was a matter of hours; God would not refuse my request.

I went out walking aimlessly, I prayed, down head and other times looking at the sky and loud. I went to a call center, I do not remember to whom I spoke when someone answered to the other side of the line, "Yes, your wife knows, she is aware of what is happening, she said that she would reach Chajarí at midnight", it sounded like a lash and punishment increased in our hearts but I had faith in God, He would give me the miracle, that I had never asked for me or for anyone. I looked wildly for a church, around a corner I found it, long and wide staircases, I walked, there was nobody, I walked to the end of the church and nobody appeared again to my encounter. I needed to talk with someone who could tell me that there was hope, I wished to be invited to ask, to pray, yes, I was afraid to do it by myself, alone. I was staring at the huge golden cross, shone with its own light and I spoke with God, He heard me and I did a deal with Him, God would heal my son leaving no marks or injuries in return of my own life, without any other considerations neither questions nor answers. It was so great to know that my faith was enormous that I felt good immediately, my head no longer ached and I could even see properly. I felt very light, free of faults and responsibilities, I even smiled. I thought when returning to the hospital my son would be waiting for me, my departure from this world would be quick, fleeting and painless, it was an exchange of one life for the other, just that, with such simplicity. I was crying again but of happiness, God was there, He existed, we had talked and even made a deal. I left the church in tears thanking God, I was filled with love, of course, I felt it, and it flowed. When I remember that situation makes me feel small, ridiculous and even ashamed of me, I was even happy to die.

I attempted to walk outside the church and a strange force made me stop, nobody held me but I could not move forward, I looked back shouting, "God, we already did and sealed a deal, let me go, please!", Nobody answered, I went back sitting on a bench, I closed my eyes and immediately began to appear images, not photos but real live images of my children who were waiting for me in Brazil and my wife looking at me with much pain and crying my departure, I felt the need to hug them and kiss them and tell them how much I love them, I needed to tell them and show them that I also loved them and I could not live without them. I quickly understood many inexplicable feelings as love, fear and cowardice, also. I got rid of the deal with God running to the hospital, I didn't feel any tiredness, I needed to talk with my son, I needed to ask him a thousand things, I needed also tell him other thousands and questions were there, not in the tip of my lips but in my heart. I felt at the same time a dreadful fear almost bordering on terror, I ran and once again approaching the hospital, I confused myself, in my thoughts.

Was darkening and cold, I went directly to the ICU, repeatedly hit the door, nobody attended, I insisted, carefully I opened the door, for respect for others patients in the same room I dressed in white and disinfected uniform from head to toe as I had seen it so many times that day and the previous day, I crossed the door. There was no one to prevent me or to stop me. Maybe about ten beds with their dying patients, all connected to noisy machines showing different numbers, graphs and colored dots. None of them spoke or coughed, just breathed, a few breathed stronger than others and machines were still making noises as playing the same music in different beat and harmony, at least the melody was the same, an opera between life and death, I could feel the difference. I slowly approached to his bed, I stopped at the foot of his bed, his body was so small for that cold hospital bed, and it was too big for him, huge. I looked at him for a long time, I wanted to order my ideas to be able to talk to my son, and I wanted to explain to him what had happened. I felt a cold wave through my body from one side to the other, I tried to follow the cold wave as if it was palpable and my eyes stopped on the neighboring bed of my son, there was lady of advanced age with her face of ash color sleeping almost peacefully, struck me such peace of mind, I was staring at her when she swelled up her lungs letting out all air that existed in her body. I knew she had died, simple, so from normal, it had been my first experience with the death, I didn't know dead, and it did not fright me. After a long time I returned my eyes to my son, I walked toward him, so fragile and helpless, I took him in my arms, I didn't care about all those wires, hoses and connections separating our bodies, I felt his body heat, I sang to him gently to his ear for long time rocking his body as when he was a baby, I felt his hug and his affection as a vibrating wave travelling between his body and mine. As a magical moment I felt peace and calm to finally talk to him in a low voice, as whispering to not bother him, came out of my interior words that I never wanted to say in my right mind, today I regret not having more faith to fight but words were born inexplicable, perhaps from my heart, I don't know. "I will explain to mom that all this was an accident, just that, a terrible accident, I will tell mom that you did not suffer, I will tell your brothers they have to be strong before any pain in life as you has faced it, we will always have you among us from far away or a beyond nearest us, you will always take care of us to ensure our existence", "My son, forgive me for my cowardice, I wanted to exchanged with God my life for yours, I couldn't, mom and your siblings will need me, it is what I understood". I love you, I love you, and I love you. I want to take advantage of this moment in its minimum fraction of the time. Nobody wants to suffer for a farewell that hurts more than an open wound but if you can't wait I will explain to mom, she is already coming, I know she will suffer and I do not know how to avoid that pain so deep, I think you are the only one that must decide when it is the time, if there is a time". He laid his head on my arm opening his hands; alarms and noises broke the magic of the moment. The huge room was filled with doctors, nurses and more people in whiter than before; also lights illuminated the space that wasn't there a few minutes earlier. I had time to hug him again kissing him in peace, he was gone forever. "Are you crazy?", said a doctor snatching my son from my arms, two others pushed me towards the door, I sat down on a long bench, there was nobody more than me and my thoughts. About an hour later a doctor came out to speak with me, we were able to stabilize him; he suffered a Cardio-respiratory arrest, "No", I said, "He has left forever, the death won, the death took him from me and he was only three years old".

It confused the emptiness of my mind with my empty stomach and even empty heart and spirit. I had a notion of time and place, nothing else, my skin seemed to be made of steel, and nothing was coming in and nothing out or emotions of others crying their own, showing nothing to anybody. I did not share what had happened with my new friends or those with whom I was travelling. I asked to take me back to Chajarí, my wife would come later. After a couple hours of travel I asked to leave me alone, they all also had their own lives; wives and children. I promised them that it would be fine taking care of myself, I just needed to be alone and rest, they agreed to leave me in a café on a road near the bus stop, I spoke with the owner of the café, I wanted to explain him what I did there without consuming anything, "It is not necessary, I know what you're going through, we all know", this is a small town", said looking at me with pain. I sat in back, there was a table for two with a large window overlooking the road, I put my hands between my legs, supported my head in the window and I got to relive the scene in the hospital, this time I saw it from the outside, I was a spectator, It seemed to feel emotional feelings of support and encouragement.

I felt when somebody touched my shoulder, before opening my eyes I felt that I shuddered, my body shook of cold, it had been a very cold night, the flames in the fireplace had consumed, steam came out of my mouth that made ice in the window's glass with the passing of the hours, it took me a few minutes to react, outside the sun appeared timidly. "You have a phone call, it is from the hospital". I crossed the road, I went to the gas station, about five or six people opened the way so I could pass through closing it behind me, everyone looked at me with curiosity and lament. "Hello?", I asked with a trembling voice. "I am sorry but your son has died", said a man on the other side of the line with the breathy voice. "Yes, I know it, last night", I confirmed without weighing the extension of my words. "No, it was a few minutes ago", corrected me the man over the phone. "Thank you", I said disconnecting the call. I knew it and I was sure of it, my son had left the night before, it was only his body which had stopped working some minutes ago, was that, a body without a soul.

Appeared immediately one of my new friends, the same that had taken me the night before, took me by my arm by putting his hand on my head to enter his car, he drove some blocks stopping in front of a small crafts business, I wanted to ask him what we were doing there but it wasn't necessary, quickly somebody opened the door and I saw my wife sitting, she looked tired and sad, disarmed, I slowly walked towards her, I knelt down with my head on her legs and I exploded in tears, her hand gently straightened my hair, she did it for a long time, I lifted my head saying, "I'm sorry, I failed, he is gone". I promised to take care of him with my life and failed". We embrace each other crying quietly, without scandals, I wanted to talk to her and tell her the details, she put her hand on my lips, and she did not allow me. "Not now, there will be an opportunity to talk". My wife had been stronger than I, looked at her and thought about the pain she was having on the inside, that the creature had come out from her guts, he was a part of her that had died, would have no words to explain, angels, from far beyond of Gods nor hopes, he was dead, it was what counted. The wound in her life that she wore was so great that her walk was heavy and the smell of blood bubbling of her body, a blood without a body but I knew that it emanated from her open heart, I just have to follow her, support her unconditionally, and no questions asked, no comments, no words.

Arriving at the hospital they told us to go to the back yard, the body of our son was in a small room of not more than seven by ten feet, the only building. He was already dressed, there were no signs of trauma, he looked calm giving us peace of mind, and he was deeply asleep. We were with him until the coffin arrived, we talked at length with him, mom told him that his brothers had been staying with grandma, she told her about her long trip from Sao Paulo to Argentina, long because she has no certainty of what she might find when arrive, she told him that by being a mother she knew that she would never see him alive, maternal instinct, she said. The Governor of the province, knowing the details of the case offered us to transport the body in a funeral car to the border with Brazil which we gratefully accepted, we'd done nothing nor had plans. Arriving to our first destination we left our son's body in the Argentinean's side; we went to a travel agency in the Brazilian's side that I already knew from before because of earlier trips I had made. The travel agent of the agency was very kind with us, giving us condolences and offering us her help, so we had dinner and breakfast thanks to her efforts. We would come out the next morning bound for Porto Alegre and then São Paulo as a final destination. We arrived at the airport, we saw that the aircraft was small, a couple of officers came up asking us if we were the parents of the dead child, once confirmed the information requested they explained us without refined subterfuge they could not load the coffin, it would be inauspicious to fly with a corpse, the passengers would not feel comfortable. The airplane did not have a specific cargo area but the tail of the aircraft, after the seats. They were unconscious and direct. We could not believe how they treated us, coldly emotions; they dealt with our son as the corpse and the passengers as someone superior to us, first class against parents who had to bury one of their children, of the second class. One of the officers in his desire for fancy righteousness apologized citing the impasse at the unusual situation, it was not normal to take a dead body on a commercial flight. Earlier the agent of the travel agency had suggested us to wrap the coffin on thick paper, brown craft paper to avoid discomforts at the airport, what we did reluctantly. "What body?, What corpse?", I asked him angrily to let my voice to rise looking at the pilot this time, "They are books!", "Do you doubt it?". "Open the box with the books", I demanded. People watched without understanding what was happening. I knew he would not be able to open the box, with books or not, he would not risk finding a corpse, we are all cowards, all of us fear of our own ghosts and shadows, I thought. "Load the box on the plane", was his final order. The flight was scary, we were flying through a big storm where the plane jumped from side to side, this type of storms are something normal in south Brazil. I hold my hand very tight against my wife's hand and constantly turning my head backwards to see how the coffin was, it was not much that I could have been done but I at least I wanted to be assured that our son was going well; even dead we wanted to vigil for his safety. The aircraft calmed down suddenly and we started to descend through the clouds until landing at a wasteland that I did not recognize, we stayed on the airplane, dropped some passengers and others got up to continue our flight.

 Hours later from the distance of our tiny windows of the airplane we could recognize a major airport, we were coming to Porto Alegre, our penultimate stop before Sao Paulo, we had to change airplanes for one larger. Off the small airplane we hoped to know details about the coffin, I asked if it would be immediately transferred to the next flight bound for Sao Paulo, "No!", Was the sour answer from the pilot, he left us watching at him and he walked away. Two officers indicated the path to be followed and this was direct toward immigration and Brazilian customs. "Why?" I asked. "The airplane did stop in Uruguay", was the unexpected answer. My wife and I ran asking to allow us to pass before than the rest of the passengers; some people allowed us, others not pushing them without pity or mercy. After that cumbersome legal process we ran without rest through the central corridors of the airport until we found the main counter of the small airline that we had traveled, for our luck or misfortune we realized that we sided with the pilot, he did not have time to be surprised and quickly we explained him that the box with the books was on its way up in customs, what would be the surprise of the people to open the box to find a corpse instead of books, now using the sarcasm in our benefit. I did not let him think nor react to follow nearly without breathing my monologue explaining that he had five minutes to take our child to a safe place or I would call a TV station, I reminded him that there are broadcasters who pay to see the curiosity and morbidity on the screens. Without options he ran almost desperately pushing many passengers in his mad race against time and against the law. We were waiting for some news with our tight hearts, our nervousness was evident, from behind the counter appeared a cargo worker asking us to follow him, we arrived at the main doors of the airport, it was mid afternoon, it was filled with buses and private vehicles, he pointed to our left side with his index finger, once we recognized the coffin wrapped in brown paper lying on the sidewalk a block away, the man ran back to the inside of the airport and the van that had brought him up to the sidewalk left swiftly. We arrived with tears in our eyes to the counter of VARIG, a Brazilian airline, I left the box on the floor, "He is our son", I wanted to explain and I could not mediate word; rage, impotence, emotion, pain and crying wouldn't let us talk. We gave our identification documents, in a few minutes we were invited to sit down. "We found your flight reservations; we will take care of you two and your son".

We had enough support from friends and relatives, in that order, when everyone returned to continue with their lives we were and felt the emptiness, many thoughts, analysis, guilt, memories, material things, toys, clothes, the looks, questions, uncertainty, worth, misery and that emptiness again with no way fill it or back to cover the space. I felt unfortunately different and unluckily special, had crashed one of the logics of life, a child's should bury their parents, in this case the parents had buried a son, and "Who responds to it?", "God knows what He does", told me all. God made all of us suffer, one by one, my son did not deserve a sample of life, he deserved a full life, as everyone he deserved a normal life, full of achievements and objectives, studies, children, grandchildren, laughter and tears, to see the trees give fruits and also pick up the leaves in autumn, enjoy his own achievements and rant to wind his failures, to take care of his parents when old and live old to a golden age. Why we deserved a special merit as such life denying his, an innocent and pure child without wickedness?, isn't the rule of life?. I didn't want to fall into conformism other people trumpeted but blame God also was a losing battle, He would never tell me and I also would never understand it, we are human and that is also a rule of life, the mystery and the unknown, lower my sight and to accept. I did not rebel against God or the saints, I never was a devout but not a pagan also, I always thought in a superior Being, a deity in the sense of superiority but not in the God of men. My life experience taught me the respect for everything and everyone, I respect those who adore a God, I respect those who profess different doctrines, and I cannot imagine the Japanese go to hell for not having a religion in particular or having a syncretism belief asking the gods and Buddha at the same time. I don't particularly believe that even the Indians before the global evangelism continue consuming in the eternal fire or even today and before, that Muslims are the enemies of Christianity and, as I remember having listened when I was only a child, everything depends of the crystal with what you see. There is no doubt that we all must believe in something or someone, because we are cowards by nature and is better to be protected against the wrath of the gods besieging beside them. I prefer to believe in the simple, in the way that life taught me and according to the actual times, in the site and the space in which I live and with the ignorance that many accuse me. "Why I cried in a different way the death of my grandmother that I loved her so much?, I continued recalling her with nostalgia and affection but I no longer cry for her. Why I cry my son's death with passion, pain and dissatisfaction? The erudite and experts may say that I have not been able to close my mourning". The wiser, erudite and doctors wouldn't give me a valid answer as neither God, it is not normal to bury a child and God could not prevent it, and is not that He did not want.

Life goes on

The years that followed were not sufficient balm to continue a normal life, as a family we connect firmly but that firmness was not enough to prevent our memory and suffering that we felt very often, not to say every day. Businesses were ultimately aside, nothing would be more important than the family; wife and children. The rest, I called simply relatives but without intent to offend, divide or belittling, they were just relatives, no family. We carry and gave away everything that belonged to our son in life; clothes and toys to a children's shelter outside Sao Paulo's city. The first visit made us feel very well, our children were amazed and we as parents with the feeling of a mission accomplished. For the second visit we took food and other toys to share with the less fortunate children and to the third visit we went empty-handed, we wanted to find out what these children wanted or needed and how we could help them. When they saw us again the children ran into our arms. Our daughter who was already five years old and our son who was a year old ran to meet them. Obviously our children sought between all kids and new friends identify any of them as their brother who was not among us, we also. It was our last visit, it was not correct to deceive ourselves, deceive our children and mislead several orphans and sick children in a fanciful reality, we knew that we could not give anything but instead we needed to receive.

A day with my adventurous zeal I threw the idea at home go to the United States of America, tourism I said, "If we go to live there?", was the counter proposal. It took not much to renew our passports, buy tickets for the trip and leave; we would stay for about six months so the tickets would be round-trip. Make plans, sell goods, hold our children's school enrollment and other thousand activities made us to divert our attention toward a new future, we would travel, we would know new places and new air, new people and their culture, a new language and its challenges. It was 1993; eleven and seven years old were already our children.

It was a long journey, direct flight from Sao Paulo to Los Angeles in California and after two extra flights we arrived in Washington State, on the West coast of the United States, twenty-four hours after having left Brazil, a veritable odyssey, we were all tired.

As welcome Washington gave us wonderful landscapes that made us remember Chile, huge mountains with snow on their peaks, rivers, waterfalls, cities of architecture renovated and fresh, much history, Indian reservations, towering green pines covering what was not built, that was what any tourist or visitor could see at first glance, simply wonderful inviting to life, to the future. We located ourselves in a small village near to a main road near the border with Canada; we rent a house with a huge yard, perhaps eight acres. I will never forget the first time snowed in our town, after an intense cold began to drop huge snowflakes, we looked from the window with great curiosity, and there were no words to decipher such magic. In a couple of hours all grass, wild flowers and our tiny garden were covered in white, to complete the landscape its finalized with the painted snow pines, everything was different, just something out of a movie, and we were the actors, we were in the middle of everything. The children stared gaping through the window's glass and my wife somewhat worried to confirm if the house would resist the weight of the snow or if the water pipes would not be frozen, my fears were the same but I did not share them. We were obviously not prepared for such a climate nor had thick clothes, heavy shoes, scarves or hats but nor would be impediments to the madness that all we were thinking and wishing, I opened the door and started running aimlessly in our giant playground, the children followed me confirming that stepping on snow was safe. We made angels lying us back in the snow moving our arms and legs as wings, we rolled in the snow, we pushed us, we throw snowballs each other and we also ate snow, it was fabulous. Within a few minutes an elk came to our backyard, it was a male and we knew it because of its huge horns, he had been hidden behind the trees, we slowly approached the animal without even importing us the danger, he jumped running in circles, we ran behind the elk as if it was a trophy, also appeared from nowhere a couple of raccoons and a skunk and a dog that later we could identify as a coyote for his howls. It was already dark and cold; it had been a fantastic, unexpected, unforgettable afternoon. It was long before I played with my children, perhaps had been the first time in this way in my life, how to forget their eyes, looking at everything with curiosity, appreciation and how grateful I was, my children had given me a great lesson and I finally understood, again. My daughter had told me during my slumber, reminding me some days after the funeral that they were also my children, I had to live for them, that I had to fight for them and mom. I didn't cry but yes, tears rolled down my cheeks, it was pure happiness.

I hold their cold hands and entered home, mom had prepared them a couple cups of hot chocolate and two cafes, one for her and one for me. We talked until late, we laugh and we remember, we also made plans for when return to Brazil and another set of plans for when we would live forever in that place, what else we could do, just dream about, it was only plans.

Years passed, they moved to different schools, other houses, the time went by very quickly, it marked the children's infancy, passed in our lives friends and also the not very closed friends, passed different jobs, the good and the bad, passed through our lives different towns and cities where we live and also it's neighbors, we were abandoning certain South Americans' traditions, what we were, our skins were permeating of this country and also of it's odd habits and customs, their meals, flavors and unpleasantness, of good people and bad people, as in all corners of this planet, as the same in my country when people are attacked by their different skin's color or different accent to ours, and mine too.

There are those who left by choice and because we could and others because they couldn't and not being able to choose. Years passed and our children without being able to choose became Americans by choice, they grew up in body, soul and conscience, today they think as they want and not as we want to. The time ran and marked, the time delimited our lives, our daughter married to a good gringo, which we respect and we love him as our own child in exchange of the unconditional love that he has given our daughter and they gave us a grandson, by these curiosities and mysteries of life, of the prior life or the afterlife he inherited the hair, lips, eyes and attitude among other attributes of his uncle, that rest in peace, whereas they do not share a single gene, human. Much we owe to our younger son, who remains alive, taut and firm in the umbilical cord of his land, which is not exactly where he was born, a Brazilian by geographical accident. We never asked them if they wanted to come or go somewhere else. Today we understand our son differently, he has the tenacity, firmness and persistence of social justice, an innate wrestler, a natural politician of magnificent understanding, of those politics we missed years ago but thanks to life we outburst him of possible politicking that has now transformed our neighborhoods, cities, countries and the world in valleys withered without human interests in exchange for percentage interests. We are certain that life a day will give him the opportunity that he deserves and seeks to participate in battles and wars where the blood would just words and wisdom, passion that he carries is not of a gringo but a life-lover and defender of hot-blooded, a Latino.

Evidently and as everyone in the world and mainly us immigrants criticize what we do not like, we disagree on what we don't want and undoubtedly we compare, it is impossible to do otherwise, it is part of our consciousness and idiosyncrasy. We adopt, we care and we change in our own way, to our way of thinking and acting what pleases us, we are creatures of habit, we eliminated certain meal's dressing and life itself to conform to our style, we are all susceptible to change, for good or for bad. We learned to like this land, with its flaws and virtues, to the American, as they want to be called, to the people themselves, to people with whom we crossed in the street, in the supermarket, in the beauty salon, in the doctor's office, everywhere and in any place, to them that little known about world geography, to them which don't care about the rest of the world as they say because are the biggest and the best, they have all the reasons to say it though this assertion distress us. They are a superior country, anyone who ever lived in these lands can't deny it, we have learned and lived the American dream, which does exist. What the American government has done outside these borders is another story and it's not up to us, to criticize, not all the American people agreed with wars or all agree with world peace, but beyond them, it is their land and it's their wealth. How to convince a gringo that a ripe fruit, sweet and fresh taken directly from a tree is better?, "It is too sweet", would probably be the answer, I tried to prove otherwise but not anymore, I also learned to respect.

Would be impossible for any Chilean, in any position or political ideology forget September 11, 1973 and every year and even more when we are outside of our country and the destiny brought us a stranger mourning that we were compelled to accept by the importance that it carried with it. Ran the year 2001 when came the attack on the twin towers in New York, I remember neatly, I turned on the television as every morning before going to work to open the doors of our small business. Instead of news I watched something different that I thought it was advertising for a new film of action, that here is normal; bombing the White House, aliens invading the Congress, terrorists staining of red the Hudson River and earthquakes wiping out the city of Los Angeles but it wasn't, it was real, commercial aircraft with people aboard with living beings who were parents, children, grandchildren, neighbors, a life, were crashing against the twin towers. We heard phone conversations on the television between passengers sentenced to die in the way less expected and terrible with their distressed relatives on the ground, people jumping from the building avoiding dying burnt.

The culmination of the tragedy was seen in slow motion, the collapse of both towers. We all knew that along with the rubble fell human beings, by thousands. Remains the discrepancy in terms of the total number of deaths among relatives of disappeared persons and the official figures, many immigrants without legal residence in the country were not registered as disappeared, many who had no family or anyone who claimed them, weren't counted as victims. Pedestrians, drivers, merchants who were around buildings also were killed, probably shredded by the millions of tons of debris that rained without prior notice. Police officers and firefighters perished in the middle of the cement powder transformed to the absolute nothing that involved the surrounding streets, volunteers, people who prayed, curious and people numb by the fear that did not know what to do in front of a nightmarish and hellish image of their own final judgment. It was a hard, painful and daunting task to begin removing pieces of body found, so destroyed, so small, so tiny and contaminated that it was impossible to catalog and identify them. Thousands of families were in need to begin to live a duel, where thousands who buried their relatives symbolically depositing clothing and souvenirs in empty coffins as reserving a place and a name in some cemetery for posterity.

This was the only time I remember having seen a country and its people so shattered, kneel down literally. They had successfully attacked directly to the heart and the spirit of this nation, land of freedom; nothing could be compared to this humiliation. I think from that September 11 the world changed, turned to what it is today, a world with its distrustful and sad people, security systems invaded the privacy of everyone, without exception, it pushed social changes and the differences, mainly religious between Catholics and Muslims, the fear to dress differently, the concern of speaking publicly saying a vetoed word. The schools' curricula renewing history, excessive use of force and power, fear to fly with people around us, to doubt of everything and everyone, to the zeal of our things, to the fear of a new neighbor or a vehicle driving twice in front of our houses, to live with racism openly, whites against Latinos, Latinos against blacks, blacks against Chinese, everything changed and we all changed. If that terrorist act had been committed against any other country the global consequences would have been superficial but not, they attacked the great elephant and we all obviously pay the broken dishes. In this country nobody, absolutely nobody was free of splinters of September 11, 2001.

New, old life

The first of August of 2012 my father died, forgiveness was immediately, I did not question myself, on the contrary, it affected me much, I cried for days and at every moment that remembered him. How it could be?, more than someone reminded me that I was becoming old, between half in jest and half seriously. My children and my wife suffered with the death of the grandfather and father-in-law, not because him but for me. I can assure you that for the first time in my life I felt the absence of my father, I felt like an orphan. I never knew conclusively if he has asked for forgiveness for something or someone but I want to believe that he did it, for him, for his sake and for his own peace to leave this world with the spiritual serenity. He died quickly, without pain or extra suffering, I don't know if happy, I know that he is no longer here among us and to complicate my existence I can assure I would like to hug him one last time, perhaps to wrap in a last hug all he owed me. He was not a good father, that I know, I don't know and I don't want to know if he was a good husband while he was married three times but this is not an area where I must say, where two people go to bed and eat two there is no space for a third party. I still try to assimilate his departure to close that great wound that I carry inside me, only time will tell me the truth. I have reviewed my life and I am not who can say if everything I did and what I do I have done well and fair. We all will be judged and we all are victims or perpetrators in one form or another, in one or other way, on the circumstances of each of us.

I can't deny my father's departure has greatly changed my way of thinking, perhaps in the short term since it is difficult at this stage of life in talking about much larger deadlines, there are moments, passages and situations in which we are more thoughtful, hesitant and analytical with ourselves, and now what?, Turn where?, Who am I?, What have I done and what I want to do? I feel the cold, winter is approaching, I need the warmth of spring and the perfume of summer, I look at the mirror and after a while with a content cry I called my wife, "Old Lady!" with affection and respect, "We need to talk". I don't know where I would be today or in what conditions If I had not had my wife by my side, there are more than thirty years of marriage in different cities and countries, with discussions, joys, sorrows and laughs, I have never forgotten we are so different, two strangers united by several feelings; appreciation, understanding, patience, love and so many more. We still walk holding our hands and we do it with pride so that everyone can see us. My wife requested that I die before than her, that way she would not leave me alone, I would not do anything wrong or do crazy things, to not suffer more and unnecessarily and I must agree, What would I do in this life by myself? I owe her everything that I am, I was born honest but she reminded me to be, I became a worker but she taught me to work harder, she made me love her as she loved me.

"Did you call me?", She asked, I answered yes, she stared into my eyes and sat down slowly as guessing that I had something serious to say, her sixth sense of woman and wife began to work, she managed to say as a complaint, "Ay, vamos lá", a Portuguese expression that we adopted, "OK, here we go". "I want to go back home?", I said. Her eyes filled with tears, her voice and posture not wavered, and she remained firm.

"Why now?", she asked. "I got tired and I want to leave, I'm afraid to die away from my land and when time passes and we're older than today it wouldn't depend on us", I explained to her with a trembling voice of emotion. "And the kids and our grandson?", she inquired. "Who wants will follow us and who stays will visit us", I said reaffirming. "How can we give happiness if we are not happy?. We need to recharge our tanks. Live for just living is not a life, we must have a reason. I want to have the opportunity to say goodbye to our people, we have buried our fathers in the distance, family and friends without the chance to say goodbye, our mothers are already octogenarian, they will then depart, we have to give them what we have denied them for so many years, love and care and the possibility of leaving a flower in their coffins, for our sake also". A couple of days later my wife came to me saying, "It is true, let's go". The decision was already taken, came a difficult part, communicating the good news to our children. In one of our Sunday's lunch and after sharing the news our daughter cried without being able to contain herself, it became difficult for her to accept our decision, it seemed to her unjust and selfish, out of what we had talked with her mother there would not be more valid arguments, we felt terribly guilty and selfish to make suffer ours but the decision was taken without any intention to harm anyone. We just thought about our happiness and prepare us for our old age, we weren't asking for too much. I was afraid to think about the mere fact of being an old dependent asking permission in somebody's house other than mine, although the home of our children but it would not be ours. They had fought for years for its physical and financial independence, we knew what they liked and what not, two sets of completely different life, we have to respect so much one as the other and it would not be us the cause of marital disagreements, from any point of view. Who marries a house wants and which is already married, well, find another place. Our son-in-law also showed his position and opinion thereon, he remained quietly looking down, his gaze was sad and he felt for his wife, who would be sad, I could read on the air and understand under conjectures.

Our daughter understood quickly, she helped us and supported us also making plans for our future, her husband had persuaded her that our decision would be the best for us and, there would be opportunities to see us, visit us and hug us. We also opened our hands much, not only material, basically we would go with our clothes and we would begin from zero, again, but on this occasion would we have to ensure the life of two, just us, bread and onion if necessary.

Our son was happy, his mother had no drawbacks to tell him, he thought and confirmed in the important thing would be for us, to see our relatives, go and visit the places that brought us memories and live on our land, eating our meals and celebrate our days. He also offered to follow our footsteps, "I'll get with you", we warned, "I want to see the world, I want to learn my language and speak a better Spanish, to know the sky which is closer to the stars, I want to know the plains and the desert, the rainy South and walk down from the mountain to the sea".

Defying my Ghosts

Made in the USA
Charleston, SC
24 December 2013